PENG

HOW TO T

Shreevatsa Nevatia is the editor of *National Geographic Traveller India*, has worked for *Hindustan Times*, *Mumbai Mirror* and *Outlook* and written for *Open* and *The Hindu*'s *BLink*.

*main ideas
important
ideas for final
comparison to others
my notes / interviews.

PENGUIN BOOKS

HOW TO TRAVEL LIGHT

HOW

My Memories

TO

of Madness

TRAVEL

and Melancholia

LIGHT

Shreevatsa Nevatia

PENGUIN BOOKS

An imprint of Penguin Random House

PENGUIN BOOKS

USA | Canada | UK | Ireland | Australia
New Zealand | India | South Africa | China

Penguin Books is part of the Penguin Random House group of companies
whose addresses can be found at global.penguinrandomhouse.com

Published by Penguin Random House India Pvt. Ltd
4th Floor, Capital Tower 1, MG Road,
Gurugram 122 002, Haryana, India

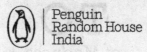

Penguin
Random House
India

First published in Penguin Books by Penguin Random House India 2017

10 9 8 7 6 5 4 3 2

ISBN 9780143440031

Typeset in Adobe Caslon Pro by Manipal Digital Systems, Manipal
Printed at Repro India Limited

www.penguin.co.in

MIX
Paper from
responsible sources
FSC® C047271

For my parents

'Write about what you know, and what do you know better than your own secrets?'
—RAYMOND CARVER

'Tataḥ kiṁ? Tataḥ kiṁ? Tataḥ kiṁ?'
What then? What then? What then?
—ADI SHANKARACHARYA

Contents

Contents

Of all the delusions that mania conjures, I find one is more enabling. I feel I remember everything. At any point, memory is at best a collection of fact and some fiction, but when I am manic, even my inventions start to seem persuasive. A psychotic subject is first an unreliable narrator. Though modern thought dictates that truth is relative, depression, which invariably follows a manic spell, leaves me lumbering with guilt. I know I have lied. I have professed undying love that I never felt. I have exaggerated my pain, and accused family and friends of crimes they had never committed. Honesty is my punishment, and so each time my life is disrupted, I keep a diary. Keeping a record, I find, makes remembering less treacherous.

I was facilitating a writing workshop in 2007 when mania first made me lose sleep altogether. 'If you haven't read Márquez, you have not had fun,' I told a group of eighteen-year-olds. Secretly, though, I had again begun to find solace in the Mahabharata and *The Sound of Music*. These were the first stories I had been told, and even though madness made linear understanding and thought untenable, it helped me identify with the protagonists. This self-importance was of course annoying, but it allowed me an immersion that, in the end, proved redemptive. By finding myself in books and films, I made sense of my condition.

I started writing this memoir six months after I had been released from a mental health institution. Lithium, therapy and the kindness of my family and friends had helped me arrive at a point where I could think without interruption. My psychoanalyst had also made a breakthrough possible. She told me, 'More than fabrication, you're prone to fantasy. The trouble with you is that you find reality boring. Trust me, it's not that bad.' Sitting across from her, twice a week, I began talking about money and food. There was suddenly more joy in the mundane than there was in Kafka. I grew averse to drama. The turbulent events of my life were best related with a smirk.

Almost ten years after I had been diagnosed as bipolar, I was no longer a victim of my affliction. Though imagined, I had seen beauty I never thought could exist. I had been to places—hospitals, Brighton and Benares—that had inadvertently made me abjure despair. Despite the discipline, the antipsychotics and abstention from marijuana, a lasting sanity could not be guaranteed. I had, however, discovered a levity that helped me laugh and love with abandon. Rather than being embarrassed by my experience, I found it had given me a few good stories to tell. Not everyone gets to think they are Shiva and Bradley Cooper.

Milan Kundera saved me when I was an adolescent and then when I was depressed. In this book, I have quoted him and others like him because it is in their writing that I have found lightness. The medicines I take every day leave my mind and body heavy. It is only in language that I discover an elusive agility. Though I am admittedly more fool than hero, bipolarity has made my many roles and my books matter.

Confession is not an act of courage. It is more cathartic than it is brave. My purpose, if I had to find one, was to play, not pander. This memoir is not a story of survival, of beating the odds or of forbearance. The only heroes of this story are the members of my support system, who, despite my recalcitrance, have stood by me and have helped me find my feet time and again. Unlike others, their names remain unchanged. They are easily identifiable. This is the story of my life as I remember it. My memories might compete with those of the people I mention, but I now have more faith in my history.

August 2017

Like Starlight in a Black Hole

On 28 February 2016, sprinting down Bombay's Breach Candy, yelling unsavoury cuss words into my phone, I missed my grandmother. When I was a boy, she'd dress me up as Krishna. In photographs she left neatly piled, I see a five-year-old with a peacock feather in his hair, mascara under his eyes, a saffron cloth tied around his waist and a flute in his hand. A row of wooden carvings on a wall of our dining room detailed the nine avatars of Vishnu. Narasimha was half-lion, far too intimidating to be emulated. For a short while, my plastic bow and arrows made me Rama, but when playing the part of my grandmother's beloved Krishna, I felt I monopolized her affection. She told me stories of him when putting me to bed. Often confused by the thievery, polyamory and trickery, I'd interrupt her with questions which now seem too human for tales that wondrous. She'd say, 'Sometimes it doesn't matter what is being stolen. You also have to see who is doing the stealing.' Pleasure and roguery, I learnt, somewhat precociously, were permissible when you were the undisputed hero of your story.

In 1988, my family invested in a colour television. The purchase was necessitated by an occasion—the weekly telecast of B.R. Chopra's *Mahabharat*. Every Sunday, I devoured an epic which despite its mature and frequent themes of sex and violence didn't come with a rating. Much like the women in my household, I'd wait to see Krishna. I would internalize the curve of his smile and the ease with which he'd beckon cows and the *gopi*s who herded them. I soon began to hold invisible mountains on my little finger and then spin the golden Sudharshana Chakra around it. My grandmother's devotion to me may have been quiet, but her adoration was conspicuous. Since my performances always had her as an audience, my pretence was never solitary.

Three years later, when I was in class three, my teacher decreed that all her students would have to enact the Passion of Christ. I might have been used to playing God, but my audition for the role of his favourite son was a disaster. I was given the part of Barabbas, a thief, who, according to Ms Pitre, was too much of a brute to form full sentences. I didn't have any lines. I just had to grunt. A group of my classmates made up the Jewish crowd who'd want me freed instead of Jesus. I was suddenly important. On the day of the play, with Jesuit priests in the front row and a stray voice shouting my name, I felt overwhelmed by my significance. I improvised. I tore my shirt on stage, beat my bare chest and, with my teeth clenched, I charged at a nine-year-old Jesus. Ms Pitre caught me by the collar when I walked off the steps, 'You just had to act mad! Now I know you really are insane.'

Beating my chest for friends, grinding my teeth for my parents and hungry for applause, I was Barabbas again. For all of February, my mania had left me sleepless, but that night, adrenaline gave way to a rare exhaustion. I curled into a foetal position on the floor and howled inconsolably. Three quick pegs of single malt had done the trick. I was asleep when my doorbell screeched at 2 a.m.

Eight people stood at my door. Five wore white coats, two looked sleepy and resentful, and the eighth, a burly bouncer, grabbed my arm and pushed me down on the bed. The man preparing an injection showed me an identity card to prove that he was a doctor. While the rest of his crew tore apart my one-room apartment, the bouncer's eyes never left me. 'We're going to have to take you for a few tests,' he said. 'Our hospital is nearby.' As his hand came to rest threateningly on my shoulder, I reminded myself of the *Mahabharat*. When Krishna goes to negotiate with Duryodhana on behalf of the Pandavas, the mercurial prince orders that his cousins' messenger be captured. Faced again with the limits of language, Krishna expectedly reveals his divine form. I smiled at my captors, and my compliance, I felt, would be proof of my sanctity. I reached for a copy of Karl Ove Knausgaard's *Boyhood Island* and asked my incarcerators to show the way. My game was not up.

In all the symbols that Hinduism uses to explain the universe, the image of a sleeping Vishnu resting on a fire-breathing snake, at the centre of an endless ocean, is, to my mind, the most terrifying. Lying on a stretcher, I stared at the ceiling of the icy ambulance. Its many neon lights soon began to resemble the roof of the cosmos. There I was, Vishnu, prostrate, awake and ready to re-establish my order. I began singing hymns I had learnt as a child. In my faltering

Sanskrit, I sang songs of my glory. The bouncer and the ward
boy began to nod off. This was my one chance for a perfect
escape, but I didn't know the terrain outside. I'd begun to
feel drowsy. I knew I wouldn't get far. Two hours later, we
stopped. It was hard to know where I was, but I remember a
bed, a drip, pills and oblivion.

admitted into hospital ~

I woke up the next morning to see that the lady on the
bed next to mine had hiked her dress to her waist, and
unperturbed by this exhibition, she was refusing breakfast.
The doctor-in-charge quickly drew the curtain, turned to
me, and in a voice sharpened to elicit shame, she asked, 'Do
you know why you are here?' I replied, 'Yes,' but then added,
'Where am I?' Starlight, she told me, was a wellness centre
and a rehabilitation clinic. 'You'll have to give us a urine
sample. We found cannabis in your home. Since when have
you been smoking that?' I was hesitant. A previous stint at a
mental health institution had taught me that honesty delays
departure. Timidly, I answered, 'One month.'

The six beds in Starlight's crammed ICU were usually
occupied. For the first two of the four days I spent in that
hot and busy room, I interrupted my silence only to plead
for a phone call. 'I was meant to start a new job on 1 March.
Please let me call my employers, please, just once.' Shailesh, a
jeweller and fellow patient in his late thirties, chuckled when
my sixth such appeal went unanswered. 'Now that we're here,
it's best if you give up want. You just need to surrender,' he
said. An alcoholic who needed a drink at 10 a.m., Shailesh had

turned himself in at Starlight. 'I had snapped at my daughter for no fault of hers. I just couldn't live with myself after that,' he confided. 'My wife said she wanted to come drop me. After meeting the doctors here, she only told me, "Serves you right."'

Jabbing a needle in several spots on Shailesh's arm, Starlight's nurses told him a vein was proving impossible to find. 'I should have smuggled in some of my chewing tobacco,' he said, looking at me ruefully. 'If I had to kill someone for a cigarette, I would,' I told him. 'But you're already in jail,' he said with a laugh. Ordered to spend the day lying in bed, Shailesh and I would pass our time playing noughts and crosses. Each time the detoxification packs in our IVs were replaced, we'd race. The first one to drain the yellow liquid would be the winner. 'You guzzle this stuff up quicker than I'd down my rum,' he once quipped. As he talked about his alcoholism, I listened to his stories of a dive bar in Borivali that hadn't once pulled down its shutters in over a decade. He confessed he was always drunk at work. Then one morning, he asked, 'What's your story? What happened to you? Why did they bring you here?' I tried sticking to the facts as I told Shailesh about the events that had led to my breakdown.

I revealed to him that, in 2007, I had been diagnosed as bipolar, and that cannabis had almost always driven me to madness. It was, however, the cheap alcohol at Bombay's Press Club that, in January 2016, proved seductive. I was sleepless, suddenly intrepid. Expectedly, perhaps, I found a comfort in the camaraderie and merriment of the club. One evening, a reporter announced he had bought a 'first-rate' packet of marijuana. He asked if I could roll. After two and a half years of sobriety, the taste of cannabis was irresistible. I soon found myself at Juhu Beach, surrounded by five middle-aged women, each wanting to sell me the marijuana they kept in bags big enough to fit a horse's head. I bought four packets. When I flew to Calcutta in February, I looked up friends who often kept a joint's worth of hash in their drawers. For those hunting for signs that'd confirm my mania, my hankering for drugs proved prognostic. I left home in the dead of night, and hours before Starlight's bouncer held me down, I'd smoked two joints and insulted my parents with rank abuse. Shailesh finally asked me, 'So, it's the insults that did you in?' Feeling contrite, I said, 'I think 2016 was an accident waiting to happen.' He smiled. 'If they'd waited, then they wouldn't be accidents.'

By the time my IV was removed, my veins had swollen. Referred to as a 'cottage' by Starlight's several security guards, my room was spartan, but I did feel thankful for its two amenities—an air conditioner and a television. I stayed inside for hours. Unable to concentrate, I'd flip channels endlessly. Once I had procured a pen and notebook, I found my writing was still manic and aphoristic. The only difference I could see was that I had started instructing myself instead of the world. I filled the book with short clumsy paragraphs. On 7 March, I wrote, 'The price I pay today is the price indiscreet men pay for excess. It isn't that a diagnosis or an addiction forbids expression. It's just that each places limits on how reformative and violent one's intent can be. A cool mind is your only ticket to sanity.' More than my manic gaffes, I now had my sentimentality to atone for.

~

Part spa and part prison, mornings at Starlight began early. Feeling inadequate after daily yoga routines, my stiff body felt too humiliated to suffer aerobics. Waiting for breakfast with a steel plate in my hand, I grew accustomed to hunger; I was too fussy an eater and the centre's food was usually insipid. I began sharing my apples with Madhava, a twenty-nine-year-old copywriter who had been unemployed for three years. Together, we'd read the newspapers, which always arrived only around noon. Delhi's Jawaharlal Nehru University was imploding with cries of sedition then, and in the days before I was brought to Starlight, I'd quoted Albert Camus on Facebook to make my protest known—'What is a rebel? A man who says no, but whose refusal does not imply a renunciation. He is also a man who says yes, from the moment he makes his first gesture of rebellion.'

'Are you feeling stupid because you were loud, or do you not believe in rebellion?' asked Madhava. Looking away, I said, 'I have never believed in parading my political opinions.' After an awkward silence, I mustered the courage to ask my new-found friend an obvious question, 'But really, why did they put you here?'

He said, 'I was still a child then. I must have been four years old. I walked into my parents' room to see my father having sex with a woman who was not my mother. I don't know if my mind kept playing tricks on me, repeating this one incident over and over, but I do believe this wasn't the only time I saw my father get intimate with that girl. I remember seeing my mother stand there, helpless, pursing her lips. I had repressed these memories for the longest time, but nine years ago, they came flooding back. My father came to hit me when I confronted him, and since then, I have chanced upon more information about his affairs. I threaten to go public, I blackmail him, and each time I do, I'm sent to one of these clinics. I may be psychotic, yes, but should my father be making life decisions for me?'

Madhava paused, giving me time to consider his question. I asked if he had told the doctors at Starlight of his predicament. 'In the first few days I was here, I cried myself hoarse. I said my confinement here was illegal. The problem is that it strangely wasn't. The "doctors" you speak of were silent at first, and later, they were just disbelieving. I have been here for two and a half months and the bill must be at least six figures. No insurance covers us, so who do you think they'll listen to, the deranged patient or his adulterous father who's coughing up the cash?' Madhava never spoke of his troubles again. He tried teaching me chess on a tattered board. He borrowed my Knausgaard, and returned it a day later, saying, 'Honesty is boring, man.' The next morning, I waited for him in the kitchen. He was late for breakfast. 'Madhava was discharged today,' a nurse told me.

~

At Starlight, you'd have to stand in queue for lunch, for your medicines, to meet the psychiatrist and, most frustratingly, to get a shave. I was used to getting in line, though. In 2013, I had spent three and a half months at Fortune Foundation, a rehab on the outskirts of Delhi. The drill of detention wasn't unfamiliar. When doctors from Fortune had come to pick me up in their van, they had found twelve packets of marijuana in my bag. 'You could've been arrested,' they said. Sitting in their farmhouse, I'd asked, 'How is this any better?'

Prisons might be too obvious an analogy for institutions that padlock their gates, but it is finally their methods which are similar. Run in accordance with the principles laid down by the founders of Alcoholics Anonymous, several group therapy sessions at Fortune required me to introduce myself again and again. 'I'm Shreevatsa and I'm an addict.' This admission never failed to fill me with shame. Disgrace was a cauldron I'd have to simmer in.

Having spent two months at Starlight, Jonathan believed that company, not isolation, was the best cure for melancholy. Joining me for a stroll, he spoke about engineering and his ex-girlfriend, but he always seemed more curious about how Fortune Foundation was run. Walking back to our rooms, he once asked, 'If you had to pick one reason why Fortune was better than Starlight, what would it be?' I didn't have to think. 'They let me smoke seven cigarettes a day.' Dissatisfied, he prodded further. 'Did you ever see any violence while you were there?' I told him about the cocaine addict who had to be restrained and the depressive teenager who broke his hip bone after he threw himself down two storeys. 'That sounds terrible,' said Jonathan, 'but tell me, did they give you shocks?' When I said they hadn't, he looked comforted. 'I wish I was there and not here,' he said with a sigh.

Jonathan asked, 'Have you noticed that I'm not always talkative, that there are days when I am very dazed and very confused?' I was quick to reply, 'But I just assumed you were depressed like me, like all of us in here.' He laughed. 'The truth is that on some mornings, I'm given electroconvulsive therapy in the ICU. They want me to forget.'

It was only in his early adulthood that Jonathan had learnt he was adopted. His biological parents, whom he soon sought out, were cold. His adoptive parents wanted him to stop asking difficult questions, and every time he was inconsolable, they'd find a new mental health facility to isolate him in. 'I can't believe a family would do that,' I said in shock. With a wry smile, he asked a question that proved brutal. 'Most of us are here because of family. Aren't you?' I felt an urge to hug him. I didn't. Then one evening, all dishevelled and numb to his surroundings, Jonathan said to me, 'They again called me in for treatment this morning. I can't take this. I don't want to know who I am.'

Initially, the journalist in me saw potential for an investigative exposé in Jonathan's torment. But later I found myself overwhelmed by fear, not solicitude. I did not want to be pinned down to a bed, seizing uncontrollably, while a nurse stuffed my mouth with rubber and another strangled my neck. Protest and surrender would then both be impossible. The confines of my room grew intolerable and I began to spend my days on a bench in Starlight's lawns. I wanted to find safety in numbers; desperate for a distraction, I tried hard to invest in banal conversation. The Jordanian Ayesha convinced me her drug habits were the effect of an unforgiving marriage, and Rahul said he had been sent to Starlight because he had fired his father's gun while under the influence of marijuana. Durga always wrote her poetry on a table nearby. I asked her why no one at Starlight ever spoke of their clinical diagnoses. I told her, 'It is almost like

Durga

mental health disorders were determined by relationships, not biology.'

Thirty-four, mother of a five-year-old boy, married to a man a decade older, Durga had a manner that was assured and charitable. 'Look at me,' she said. 'The doctors here have told me that I have a personality disorder. I like to think that it's a fancy way of saying I don't fit in, but then I consider the symptoms—difficulties in personal relationships, trouble functioning in society. That describes me perfectly. So, which came first, biology or relationships? I'll say it was the chicken.' Durga knew how to make her audience smile. Our conversations lasted hours. She would surprise me with quips that were as profound as they were flippant. 'I love Shiva,' she started telling me one day. 'He is my god, but why did he have to go and become so fashionable?' I asked, 'So your problem is not that you're a fanatic, you're more worried you're a groupie?' Her giggle was childish.

The day her husband came to visit her with their son, Durga looked unusually sullen. At the end of each day, she'd read out to me the poetry she had scribbled, and I would anxiously share my realizations. I had grown used to our little writing workshops. 'Today, I only have an aphorism for you,' she announced when I sat down next to her. 'You're stepping into my territory,' I warned, trying to make her laugh. 'The difference between regret and remorse is simple,' she went on. 'Regret makes you change your mind, while remorse requires a change of heart.' For a few seconds, I considered the poignancy of her sentence. 'Spoken like a true poet, but I must ask, are you all right?' She looked away when saying she wasn't.

Earlier that afternoon, when she was trying to build blocks with her son, Ayan, in Starlight's office, he kept running to his nanny, closing his arms around her neck. Durga said she didn't have the courage to tell her husband she was jealous. 'I hired her, and now I don't want to see her face again. You'll probably find this all very silly, but for the first time, I hated myself for ending up here. I don't blame my son. He is looking for an affection that is constant and I can't give him that. He'll just grow up to resent me. I will be the mother who was never there. So yes, here's my fear. My son will hate me.' I didn't feel empathetic instantly. I just felt pleased to have become Durga's confidant. 'But almost all sons hate their mothers. No matter how hard she tries, a mother can never be there enough,' I said.

She wasn't consoled. She said, 'But surely sons feel they have let their mothers down too.' I'd again found an opportunity to explain my guilt, and I wanted to relate to her one moment that had defined it. I started by saying, 'I was in Brighton—' but Durga cut me short. 'Brighton? Fancy! How did you end up there?' I told her I was twenty-three at the time, in love with a woman who was British and fourteen years older. 'She had a daughter who was seven. I wanted to return to Britain to be closer to a family that had chosen to call me theirs,' I said. 'Fourteen years older,' Durga exclaimed. 'We do have a lot in common. So, what happened then?'

It was with relish that I spoke about the months I spent at the University of Sussex in 2008. 'I was having the time of my life. My professors and the weed were both excellent. True to form, though, I went manic. I had stopped sleeping. I was calling people in the middle of the night. I was being inappropriate. I impulsively took a flight to Delhi. My cousin Rana met me at the airport and took me to a hospital that housed more addicts than the infirm.' Like Jonathan, Durga too wanted to compare Starlight's care to that of other mental health institutions. 'This might not be good,' she said, 'but there is some comfort in knowing that it is better.' She was an attentive listener. 'The Delhi hospital,' I said, 'was more a nursing home than a Starlight-like sanatorium, but Dr Makhija, the psychiatrist, didn't know what he was doing. My body rejected his medication, and I just drooled.'

I told Durga of the day I freed myself from the restraints that had kept me tied to a bed. Catching the security personnel off guard, I had climbed the hospital's high gates. The spikes had scraped my thighs and the barbed wire bruised my palms. A man running at full throttle is conspicuous. It didn't take long for six burly men to drag me back down the street. 'I soon became catatonic,' I said. I was expecting Durga to show pity, but she only asked if the hospital offered any therapy. 'I was once put in a room with two counsellors who thought a close reading of *Men Are from Mars, Women Are from Venus* would calm me down.' For the first time that evening, Durga laughed heartily. 'You must have had a field day,' she said. 'I quoted feminists like Jacqueline Rose and Judith Butler,' I confessed. 'I was so contemptuous. I am still embarrassed about that, but I felt a greater regret after I was released from that hospital. That's when I knew I'd let my mother down.'

Dr Makhija, I told Durga, had left my parents with a bill that had quadrupled in three weeks, but my parents' concern was not monetary. Once we returned to Calcutta, my mother tried to include my father in an 'intervention'. She asked me,

'What about all the drugs they found in your system?' The topic was unsavoury and my father was quick to deflect: 'It only added to his suffering. Let's not talk about it.' I confessed to Durga that this open acknowledgement of my drug habit had mortified my mother. 'But even though your cover was blown, you still kept smoking marijuana?' There was curiosity in Durga's question, not judgement. 'Yes, and I sometimes used her money to buy drugs,' I admitted. 'My father has always been supportive, and my mother has only been kind. When I yelled at them before I was brought here, my mother said she was suffering palpitations. I have to make amends. I am desperate.' Durga patted my head and said, 'We are mothers, not sons. We forgive.'

~

Nikhil, a hypnotherapist and counsellor, conducted weekly sessions at Starlight that were animated. Unlike his colleagues, he wore jeans and never shaved his stubble. 'If someone wants hypnotherapy for something that might have been bothering them, you can meet me for a one-on-one session this afternoon,' he said. I was quick to sign up. 'I want my parents to forgive me,' I told him.

'I can only prepare you for forgiveness.' His tone was detached, yet sympathetic. Taking me outside, he took out a crystal from his pocket. As he tried to swing it between us, the stone oscillated wildly. 'Sometimes this is a sign. You might not be ready for hypnosis.' I was crestfallen. 'There is one other option,' he continued. 'Go leave your shoe at the other end of this ground.' I did as I was told. I was befuddled by his next instruction. 'Now go back and walk to this shoe with your eyes closed. Think about what you want.' The sun beat down on us, and as I walked, one bare foot on the hot gravel, I felt duly repentant. When I reached the shoe I had left behind, Nikhil asked me to wear it. 'What do you feel?' he asked. 'Relief,' I replied. 'But do you feel forgiven? Do you feel as if *you* have forgiven?' 'No.' I was honest. He said, 'But you're in your parents' shoe. Now you know how difficult it might be for them.' The exercise only left me wrecked.

~

The depression that follows a spell of mania is devastating and inevitable. In the days before I was brought to Starlight, the world was a cornucopia of possibility. I had a plan that would make me a millionaire, and those who loved me would only get richer. Now suddenly I had no future, and having spent all my savings in a bookshop, I had no money. I told Durga I felt unemployable: 'I don't have any more cards that will get me out of jail free.' When I felt deserted by language, I wouldn't write in my journal, and Durga would gently let our conversations peter out after a few pleasantries. But Starlight, a theatre with many characters and no protagonists, didn't always allow for soliloquies. ✕ narrative fiction for detachment

Surrounded by a green valley, the rehab did offer scenic escape, though, and I'd found that its garden patch was mostly unvisited. One afternoon, I sat staring at a hibiscus plant, when Ishan interrupted my reverie. Ever since I had seen him twist his lanky, limber body in our morning session of yoga, I had been envious. He'd always wear a Bart Simpson

T-shirt and a bowler hat. I'd never have his swagger. 'I just heard that you and I are both from Calcutta,' he said, 'and that we are both here for smoking marijuana. What are the chances?' I wasn't feeling sociable, and in a dismissive tone, I said, 'It's a small world.' Impervious to my response, Ishan promptly went looking for a chair.

Sitting down, Ishan asked where I lived in Calcutta, and soon enough we were discussing the traffic and food of the city. He said, 'I like to think of Calcutta as a retard, brother. It's so slow.' I couldn't help but frown when I replied, 'I think retards and Calcuttans would both find that offensive.' Ishan said his father owned a textile business. 'But three years ago, when I was twenty-seven, I decided I would never work again. I only want to enjoy myself. Isn't that what life is for?' I was amused by his hedonism and entitlement.

Though I was finding it hard to indulge Ishan's callowness, our home town was not the only thing we shared in common. Like me, he too wanted to correct the past. Two months earlier, Ishan had travelled to Europe with four of his friends. He described, in some detail, the orange dust that would settle on his fingers after he crumbled the hashish he bought in Amsterdam's cafes. High on magic mushrooms, he had jumped into the sea from the balcony of his Barcelona hotel room. His stories sounded fantastic. He asked after some time, 'Have you ever been to Europe? How did you travel around, flights or trains?' Unable to tolerate his pompousness any longer, I replied, 'I went all around on a rocking horse. I travelled the whole world while staying put in Calcutta.' I felt guilty as Ishan rose to leave. 'You're funny, brother,' he said, 'I hope you see we're not that different, you and I.' I could only smile. He had begun to walk away when he turned and asked, 'How did you lose your pot virginity?' I answered, 'I was nineteen and it was all thanks to a friend.'

Once I was alone again, staring at the hibiscus, I chastised myself. I had not been able to disguise my own cockiness, and worse still, I was feeling competitive. I had gone to Britain only to study, but I felt I could have told Ishan a story that would have proven I too was worldly, if not as well travelled. I wanted to call him back and say, 'I want to answer your last question again.' beginning of addition ——

I was nineteen when I first smoked marijuana in 2003, I'd start. Sam, a self-confessed 'stoner', drove his car to the middle of an empty field and passed me a bong he carried with him at all times. I inhaled and almost immediately I was coughing and spluttering, holding tightly on to the dashboard. A few minutes later, I thought the stillness around me was audible. Pictures of the Cornish landscape, marked by ragged cliffs and a crystal sea, had brought me to Falmouth College of Arts. But it was then that I found in its green lushness an unknown magnificence. Sam handed me a sandwich, and before my terrible paranoia set in, he and I giggled like schoolboys. The clumsiness of a seagull was enough to leave us guffawing. For the first time, I had talked to a Westerner without an awareness of my cultural difference. Drugs became a gateway, my ticket to assimilation.

My college had furnished my tuition fee, and three benefactors in Calcutta helped me pay my rent. The little money I earned from odd jobs—a cashier at a grocery store, a bouncer at music festivals, a busboy in a castle's cafe—was all given to my dealer, who brought me marijuana in carefully folded bags. My fingers grew dexterous, and my newly acquired skill of rolling joints endeared me to classmates whose *Monty Python* and *Blackadder* humour had, until then, been impenetrable. Shevy, my invented double, wore clothes that were too large for him and, mysteriously, always had 'stuff'. He spent his time sitting in cemeteries and walking to the lighthouse. He could not say much about the music he always listened to, but he was self-sufficient.

In the summer of 2003, my girlfriend and I broke up on the phone. I lost my grandmother later that year, and my late adolescent response to these tragedies was insobriety and starvation. My diet quickly reduced itself to bread and butter with a ready supply of cannabis. I only spoke in class, and my addled mind grew embittered. When a drunken white supremacist held me by the collar and assaulted me in the corner shop where I worked, I saw in the violence a racist agenda that was implicitly furthered in the classroom and in academia. The campus counsellor prescribed Prozac, and gave me a letter to extend submission deadlines for essays. My ennui had a name—depression.

The marijuana I smoked with my Prozac focused my mind. Studying literature and media studies, my curriculum included third-wave feminists, Freud and Foucault. I articulated my otherness in terms that were postcolonial and psychoanalytic. The joints I smoked, the cocaine I sometimes snorted and the magic mushrooms I ingested all sent me back to a room that was stuffed with books and A4 sheets of paper. I didn't have to have conversations. I could make them up. The fiction I wrote at the time, pages of unattributed dialogue, read more like scripts I'd written for theatre. I celebrated my graduation with cannabis. I climbed the ruins of a bell tower. I really wanted to jump.

~

The 2013 Mental Health Care Bill includes in its definition of 'mental illness' all 'mental conditions associated with the abuse of alcohol and drugs'. It isn't clear if the Indian state views substance abuse as a cause or effect of mental disorders, but in institutions like Starlight Wellness Centre—de-addiction clinics that double up as mental health facilities—a history of drug use can eclipse the repercussions of more crippling afflictions. The day I was assigned a psychotherapist, I tried hard to explain to her that an emotional turbulence had often forced me back to marijuana. Internment, she reminded me, was the consequence of that action. The medicines I was being administered were enough to tackle my bipolarity. Drugs were evidence of volition. I was damnable because I had surrendered to temptation.

Though I found her supercilious, I'd anxiously await the fifty-odd minutes Dr Madhuri Sen gave me every week. I was in my room one Wednesday, completing a list of the topics I'd like her to discuss, when I was called in for my third session. Seeing two other people in her room, I turned to leave. 'We were all waiting for you,' said Dr Sen, in an effort to stop me. She handed me a textbook and asked me to read aloud a chapter that described the effect drugs had on the brains of American adolescents. Rajan, who was listening intently, protested midway. 'I've never done things like heroin. This doesn't apply to me.' Dr Sen replied in an irritable voice, 'But you smoked marijuana. That's the first step to these harder and more harmful drugs.' Once I'd finished, the three of us were quizzed individually. Since addiction itself is juvenile, addicts are very easy to infantilize.

Stepping out of Dr Sen's room, I looked dejected. Cyrus, who'd spend his days sitting in the foyer outside, looked at me and said, 'You do know that I undo in five minutes what they do in fifty.' The top two buttons of his shirt were undone. Wearing glasses I badly wanted to clean, Cyrus, a stout man in his early fifties, couldn't have seemed more avuncular. 'There are so many things I'd have liked to talk about. Now I just feel like a frontbencher who was asked to read in class,' I told him. Cyrus's laugh sounded more like a throaty gurgle. 'Sit down,' he said. 'What are these things you want to talk about?' Though I feared he was making me his afternoon's entertainment, I sat in the plastic chair next to his and pulled out the list of concerns I'd prepared for my therapist. 'I wanted to tell her how I did not want to become an object of pity or ridicule. I wanted to say all I want is respect and, if I am lucky, some worth.' Cyrus stared at me for a second or two before exclaiming, 'Boy, you sound depressed! What are you here for?' I was looking at the floor when I said, 'I'm bipolar.' He smiled again. 'And you were caught smoking up?' I nodded. 'Well, you and me both, kiddo,' he said.

After being diagnosed manic-depressive in his late twenties, Cyrus said he spent much of his time looking after his ailing mother. 'We lived in a large bungalow. I have three siblings, two sisters and a brother. We each had our own room, and I guess the house just had too much space for there to be any real intimacy. It really was very big.' Once his brother had moved out and his two sisters had left for the States, Cyrus said the only witnesses to his capricious mood swings were his mother's nurse and her chiropractor. 'I was caring for someone,' he said. 'I had reason to manage my bipolarity better. But then I started self-medicating with cannabis. I exhausted all my second chances with my brother—he didn't give me too many—and soon I started to spend more time in mental health institutions than at home. I have been here for two years, and I know that for my family, it comes down to property in the end, but I miss my mother. I should be with her now.' Cyrus see-sawed between fortitude and hurt when he spoke, and then he suddenly lowered his voice to add furtively, 'I've written a memoir. I'm looking for an agent. You know anyone?' I said I'd give him a few names. Feeling curious, I then had to ask, 'Why a memoir?' He replied with some resignation, 'So I won't have to explain myself over and over again.'

Scared that I was peeking into my future, I listened with rapt attention to the story Cyrus had to tell. He, though, seemed more interested in *my* past. He asked if I remembered how I felt when I was manic for the first time. 'It felt like an awakening,' I said instantly. 'I felt like I was Krishna. I felt I was the Second Coming. When I read Márquez by my window, I thought he was whispering *One Hundred Years of Solitude* in my ear. And then things got ugly. I was offending friends, not mystifying them. I left my parents' home with only books and a toothbrush, and soon I ended up on a hospital bed to hear a doctor tell me I was bipolar.' After a long silence, Cyrus finally said, 'And I'm sure you never believed him.' I was now feeling talkative. 'No, I didn't. A friend told me that my mania could have been a one-time psychosis, and when I wanted to smoke marijuana again, I believed her.' Cyrus said with a wry smile, 'It always gets us in the end. I'd tell myself weed helps me stay calm when manic, that it helps me do things I need to do when depressed. But here we are.'

Having lied to my doctors in Calcutta about my continued drug use, I told Cyrus I felt disconsolate. 'For seven years, they have been patient with me. They've given my language credence, not my symptoms. They did not deserve to be deceived. If I'd told them I had taken to marijuana again, I wouldn't be here.' Cyrus then said, 'But is it the marijuana that you were after or the mania? I know I have always wanted to feel invincible. That's the seduction.' I must have still sounded piteous when I said, 'What good is that invincibility? I am not God, nor am I Naipaul. I'm just a lousy hack who has been put in his place.' Cyrus straightened up. 'Never discount your mania,' he warned. 'If you won't stop to learn from it, you'll never understand its appeal. And pity will only take you that far. At some point, you'll have to take a leap of faith.' Again inconsolable, I asked, 'So you're essentially asking me to jump off a cliff?' Cyrus remained unaffected. 'All I am saying is that there's a trampoline at the foot of that mountain. You need to go jump a little. You need to have some fun.'

Sitting outside my room the next day, I was staring at the trees in the distance. They had begun to combust. Watching this sight of destruction, I thought of children whose shirts may have accidentally caught fire. I was waiting for the flames to reach my doorstep. Walking out of the cottage next to mine, Cyrus laughed at my anxiety. 'You're being paranoid.

That's just some farmer burning his straw. Your problem is you want to die, and you don't have the balls to do it yourself.'

I thought of the list I was making for Starlight's therapist. I said, 'I know what my first question to Dr Sen will be. How do you ensure a happy death?' Cyrus looked at me compassionately. 'Didn't you hear? She is on leave for a fortnight. You have me until then, though.' I felt betrayed. I said, 'So riddle me this, doctor. How do I stop berating myself for my mania?' Cyrus then squatted in front of me and said, 'The problem is you have an honest self, and that I think is you right now. You also have an ideal self, someone you thought you were when you were manic. You can do what your honest self wants to do or what your ideal self would have you do. The choice is yours. All I'll say is that you should choose wisely, kiddo.'

~

In Shailesh, Jonathan, Durga and Cyrus, my sorrow had gradually found a community. Unlike Starlight's administrators and therapists, their response to my grief was warm, almost novelistic. Empathy, for them, came naturally. They didn't have to invent their kindness. Even Colonel Subramanian, a retired army officer, came up to me to say, 'I have your back. After today, you will walk with me.' For the colonel, conversation and confession were counterproductive. 'All this talking,' he said, 'only makes you remember what you should forget. What matters is physical fitness.' Colonel Subramanian, Jonathan told me, was here because his wife had had enough of his long tryst with the bottle. While trying to keep up with the army man, I never once brought up his alcoholism. He walked with a stride that was regal, and my steps were comparatively oafish. It took me just three days to give up. I went up to him to say, 'I can't walk, Colonel. My tummy is cramping.'

A week later, I finally couldn't avoid him any more. Every once in a while, patients at Starlight were asked to talk about their professions. On that Wednesday, I had little idea I'd be sharing the stage in Starlight's recreational room with Colonel Subramanian. He went first, and after he had talked about his time at the border, I felt I needed to match his valour. I bragged about the times I had been parachuted into Afghanistan and Lebanon. 'And then there was Egypt in the Arab Spring,' I boasted. I talked about the joy of giving headlines, turning a perfect sentence and meeting people who would otherwise never have opened their doors. Seeing my audience become impatient, I added shamelessly, 'I even interviewed Deepika Padukone and Ranbir Kapoor.' Three fellow inmates soon cited headaches as their reason to leave. Two had already slipped out, and Sahil, a neurotic man in his late forties, sat near the door, his hat on his face, lightly snoring. I could tell it was time to wrap up. I ended with a line I'd written with deliberation. 'On some days, you feel you have ruffled a feather or two. Those few days, for me, have been the happiest.' No one applauded. Jayant, the amiable counsellor, looked at me and said, 'You've had such an interesting life, Shree.' He turned to the five people in the room. 'Come on, a big hand.' The slow clap was no consolation.

The main hall of the wellness centre was circular. Every morning, its patients would gather around on sofas to sluggishly recreate an interpretation of Dante's concentric Inferno. Jayant would stand in the centre, and lead his half-comatose audience in prayer. We'd sing popular devotional songs from Hindi films, and I'd keep my eyes trained on Amrita, a twenty-eight-year-old fashion designer, whose religious ardour was captivating to watch. Jayant would then choose the day's topic and ask each of us to share our views on themes that ranged from discipline and forgiveness to patience and self-control. On some days, he would also assign weekly duties. 'Responsibility helps rehabilitation. You're always reading. You can be the librarian,' Jayant told me.

The rehab's library, principally a collection of books that had been left behind by former inmates, fit into a single cupboard. The illustrated Mahabharata was deemed too bulky to borrow. 'That's a reference book. Only for library hours,' said Jayant. 'But, sir, library hours are for only one hour, and on most days, the key to this room can't be found,' I pleaded. 'Then just look at the pictures,' the French-bearded Jayant replied with a laugh. A Sherlock Holmes omnibus was just as thick, but the counsellor agreed it was dog-eared enough for me to take back to my room. To a depressed mind and to an imagination that is too parched to predict the twist of a whodunnit, Arthur Conan Doyle can be restorative.

I sat in that library every day, waiting to lend out the other spiritual, self-help and crummy fiction titles Starlight offered, but there were almost no takers. Another cupboard stocked books on psychology, tomes that all seemed to have illustrations of the human brain on their covers. 'Those are only for us counsellors,' Jayant warned.

Evanescence, or an intimation of it, can make time bearable. The cliché of 'this too shall pass' can bring solace even to those suffering an otherwise debilitating depression. But in Starlight, where I was denied even the one token phone call, the world outside had died. My incarceration seemed like exile, and since exile is by its very nature sentimental, I grew nostalgic about a home I was convinced I'd never return to. Durga and I spoke about love. Cyrus and I talked about language and its new limits. We tittered together when a social worker came to test our general knowledge by asking us to name India's states and their capitals. Aditi, who was training to be a doctor at Starlight, once asked me, 'Is there anything you'd like to talk about?' I said, 'I'd like to talk about loss.' She was quiet for some time, and then said chirpily, 'We have a lot of activities here. I'll ask Jayant to give you a part in that skit he is directing.'

'There is no script,' Jayant told me. 'You'll have to improvise.' The narrative of his play was simple. A wife in her late thirties finds herself pregnant. Her husband is drunk when she informs him of this. In his stupor, he pushes her against the floor. I was asked to play their marriage counsellor, and I was told I had to stress the repercussions of alcoholism. I fumed against domestic violence instead. 'I like how forceful you were. You're a natural,' said Jayant, slapping my back after the performance. At Starlight, it didn't take long for adults to slip into an attitude they had renounced when they left school. The inmates all divided themselves into groups, and loyalties were constantly tested and forsaken. If a man chose to walk with a woman, whispers grew loud. Shailesh became the class comic, and I the teacher's pet.

On 22 March, World Water Day, I wore black and pretended to be a tap and shower that were carelessly left running by the young who disregarded conservation and its benefits. My face seemed unrecognizable in the mirror. The chalk powder had made it spectral and white. The loud, red lipstick made me look like a clown who, for good reason, was now a universal object of fear. It was ironic that my ghoulishness took all of fifteen minutes to rinse off. Aditi asked if I could help her with email addresses of journalists who'd be interested in featuring our environmentally conscious efforts. I saw my ghastly form in the pictures she wanted sent. I gave her addresses that were never checked.

One evening, Jayant gave me the task of editing Starlight's first in-house magazine. Durga wrote a few poems, and, glad to again be trusted with a laptop, I sat to congratulate Starlight for achievements I carefully invented. The bouncer who had burst into my home was suddenly compassionate. The reticent doctors became beneficent. The facilities were ace. Psychiatrists who gave you just two minutes of their day were remarkably perceptive, and my counsellors began to resemble paragons of empathy. I was lying through my teeth. The fiction mellowed my resentment.

~

April proved benevolent. Still wistful, my journal entries grew lighter. On the first of the month, four weeks after being brought to Starlight, I had written, 'I am depressed and that's the sad truth of it. It will take some picking up from here, but if the weather conditions stay stable, I hope we will be fine.' I had followed this up with an obituary to a fly that was resting on a window of the World Trade Center on 11 September 2001. Feeling more buoyant, I sat in Starlight's kitchen, gulping down an unpalatable breakfast. A new patient sat at the other end of the table, her hair a mess, holding a copy of Swami Vivekananda's biography. Suddenly, she began shouting. 'You, what are you so afraid of? If you have it, why won't you show it?' She was looking in my direction. She was talking to me. 'Stop being scared, you crook.' My fear, I felt, had started to reek. I left my banana uneaten and walked back to my room.

On the night of 5 April, I dreamt my sister and I were sitting on a hill. Beneath us was a pile of our clothes, and we spoke like children. 'You can't tell Mum and Dad about what I've done,' I was pleading with her. Four years older and fiercely watchful, she replied, 'Only if you don't plan to do it again.' My feet then became two-dimensional. 'You're the gingerbread man,' my sister exulted. Slowly, I could feel my body turn to biscuit. My face was all I had left. I feared I was going to die. I jumped off the hill, opened the door to my room, and ran down the passage that bordered Starlight and the valley. By the time I had reached its end, I felt my skin beginning to restore. I woke up. I was startled, expectant of freedom.

The next morning I was told that Dr Sen had resumed her duties and that she wanted to see me. A few minutes into our session, she asked, 'What is the one feeling you feel most strongly?' I didn't have to think. 'Anger,' I replied. 'Who do you feel angry towards?' she asked. 'I first feel anger towards myself. My actions have brought me here, and not a day goes by when I don't wish I had done things differently. And I feel angry that my parents put me here. I understand the

dictatorial kindergarten!

reasons why I had to be incarcerated, but was this dictatorial kindergarten the only option?' Something inside me was beginning to thaw. For the first time in five weeks, I felt tenacious. 'You also feel angry with me,' Dr Sen said with a half-smile. I stuttered. 'Think about it. You do,' she went on.

That day, Dr Sen spoke to me about my future. She asked, 'What do you want to do most with your life?' My answer had remained the same for two decades. 'Write, but this time I'd like to see if I can write well.' She pressed on. 'What do you think about living in Calcutta?' I answered promptly. 'That might be a fate worse than this.' She was curious. 'Why would you say that?' I was categorical in my dismissal. 'Calcutta is the hell where nothing ever happens.' Her manner didn't change when she added, 'Your parents will be coming to see you today.' I tensed up, overwhelmed by hope and guilt. 'Are they coming to take me away or visit?' Dr Sen said, 'Visit.'

For the next hour, I paced the grounds of Starlight. Five weeks earlier, when I had spoken to my parents, I had been indignant. I had accused them of crimes they had never committed. I had hurled abuses I'd picked up from the street. No apology, I was convinced, could ever suffice. When I walked into Dr Sen's room again, I was expecting a couple that sat with their arms crossed, distant and irate. My father met me with an embrace that lasted a full minute. My mother's eyes were moist, and when she asked me how I was, her voice was choked. I mumbled I was sorry. My father playfully hit me on the head and said, 'Bunshi, I think it might finally be time to shut it. It's so good to see you.'

Dr Sen interrupted our emotional reunion and said this might be an opportunity for family counselling. I was asked to tell my parents what I'd want from them. 'Space,' I replied. 'It's been a torrid few weeks, and I think I'll just need some space to recover.' Dr Sen looked to my father. He hesitated before saying, 'We'd like Shreevatsa to live in Calcutta. That's where, I think, we can support him best. That's where his doctors are.' My mother went on to add, 'The last time, he used language that really hurt. I wouldn't want to hear those words again.' Dr Sen proposed that I repeat exactly what I had said. Suddenly a union, all three of us exclaimed, 'No!' Once the counsellor had again explained to me the benefits of therapy, my father said, 'We'd like to take Shreevatsa home.'

The permissions didn't take long to come. Helping me pack my belongings, my father said, 'You really scared us this time.' I said, 'I think I scared myself, Pops.' He asked, 'Never again?' I nodded.

The goodbyes were hurried. I later felt embarrassed to have been so giddy with excitement. I thanked Durga for listening. 'Take care of that head, boy,' she said, while giving me a quick hug. Cyrus tipped an invisible hat. For days I had been wearing pants and a T-shirt that were a size too big. My mother had brought with her a shirt and a pair of jeans that finally fit. I felt too sorry to ask my father what the figure was at the bottom of Starlight's receipt. I detailed for my parents the sum of my days. My recollections made me laugh. I asked them to stop the car when I saw a man selling cigarettes. The alcohol interceptors I'd swallowed made nicotine taste metallic. I used my mother's phone to call a friend. 'Free at last,' I told her. 'They freed Jesus this time, not Barabbas. Meet me. I'll show you my cross.' She laughed. 'You were always my little drama queen.'

affectionate parents
~~too~~ alof hospital

2

Free Love and Other Stories

College

I first arrived in Falmouth on a cold January night in 2003. The town was bathed in the orange of street lights, and at half one in the morning, it was altogether deserted. The Cornwall I had seen in the Falmouth College of Arts prospectus—cliffs dropping into an electric-blue ocean, pristine beaches, a prismatic pier—was one I would still have to imagine. A liaison officer from the international office led me up the steps of an apartment block the college had allotted to first-year undergraduates. The room I was given resembled a Scandinavian prison cell. The desk, cupboard and narrow bed left little space for me to walk.

My four housemates were white and they were all women. With most pleasantries exhausted, I started watching *Sex and the City* in the hope of further conversation. Unfortunately, I couldn't hide my contempt for Carrie Bradshaw. As the only student in my class who wasn't British, I tried hard to compensate for my otherness with my accented volubility, and the only man who befriended me was the thirty-nine-year-old Ethan. He liked drinking every day, so we made a Falmouth pub our regular joint. Ethan was the oldest in our batch and said he knew my alienation well. After the first few drinks, our conversation would have an inevitable destination—the hardships of long-distance love. He had a girlfriend in Wales and I had one in Calcutta. One Saturday, he told me, 'I wish they'd see what it is like for us. We're the ones who go away. We're the hunters. We're at sea.'

Mallika   Mallika was not amused when I recounted this conversation to her. It had been a while since she stopped being amused by things I said. Before leaving for Falmouth, I had suggested to her that we break up. Four months away from her in 2002 had made me realize that the bridge between late adolescence and a new adulthood is rickety. Before I left, we decided that I was being hasty. A togetherness of two years was too cherished to forsake for abstract inevitabilities. Relatively alone, feeling wistful and foreign, I felt glad when calculating time in accordance with the Indian standard. I'd impatiently wait for the hour she'd come online. I grew reliant on the Internet for my well-being.

My chats with Mallika, warm at first, soon grew discordant. My loyalty to our relationship had been put in question. We fought almost every day, and though I could still lay claim to a precarious intimacy, I could not correct the dissonance. I had spent my life saying sorry for faults, both real and imaginary, but my apologies now came from a place of resentment. No matter how earnest or regretful I'd sound, Mallika couldn't be softened. I grew tired.

One day I thought I'd found a way out of this impasse. I would have to transform myself from an object of loathing to one of pity. I used the name Dr Jane Allsopp to create a new email address, and pretending to be Falmouth College of Arts' campus counsellor, I sat down to write to Mallika. I apologized for my unusual mail. Doctor–patient confidentiality is sacred, and the very fact that I was mailing her could well be considered a breach of trust. Circumstances, sadly, had forced my hand. Dr Allsopp wrote that Shreevatsa had come to her in a state that could best be described as despondent.

Even though it might be too early to arrive at a diagnosis, Dr Allsopp's medical sense made her think that Shreevatsa was either partially schizophrenic or suffered a borderline personality disorder. Trying to perfect the voice of my invented therapist, I told Mallika about the affection I had for her, about how our constant friction might perhaps be taking a toll on my mental health, about how I was in sore need of compassion and care. Dr Allsopp told Mallika her email address had been procured surreptitiously for a reason. In therapy, confidence is hard to win, and any evidence of its loss could permanently stifle my future progress.

Mallika's reply was prompt. Her concern, carefully articulated in a few paragraphs, first overwhelmed me and then heightened the terrible guilt I felt. My betrayal was too unscrupulous to confess. Though I had laboured to make my fiction watertight, I had in fact never visited a therapist or counsellor. I gave myself my very first diagnosis, and even if the afflictions I had attributed to my mind were exaggerated, I suspected an inevitable comeuppance when I was told I was bipolar four years later. As a seventeen-year-old, wanting to emulate Ernest Hemingway and Sylvia Plath, I had told Mallika I wished I were mad. Love ensures wish fulfilment, yes, but in my case, it even facilitated clairvoyance.

Male
Chatroom

Jane Allsopp wasn't the first woman I'd conjured. When I was fourteen, I had discovered the pleasures of adult chat rooms. It didn't take long to learn that male usernames hardly ever attracted attention. Women, on the other hand, would be inundated with requests. I started identifying myself as Trixy, Julianne and Courtesan. In order to perpetuate the charade, I stressed the details. I said I had a birthmark on my right arm and a tattoo on my lower back. Role-playing as a nurse, secretary, hitch-hiker and masseuse, I befriended users who claimed to be Aaron, Dave, Punk Princess and Ms Bambi. Anticipating what would later come to be a New Age cliché, F. Scott Fitzgerald had once written, 'For what it's worth: it's never too late or, in my case, too early to be whoever you want to be.' For the better part of my adolescence, I found in those chat rooms a freedom that Fitzgerald had endorsed.

In rooms such as 'The Hospital', 'Home Alone' and 'Ladies Only Lounge', users are asked to provide along with their names a picture that websites rather suitably call 'avatars'. But it is invariably language that helps you establish an identity. The rules of reality, as a consequence, aren't completely absent. For me, the Internet soon reduced gender to a game of hoopla. The words I used as hoops could fall on any self that I was then invited to inhabit. Deception was based not on who I was, but on what I said.

deurtron, new IP

~

Bipolarity, I understood somewhat belatedly, does not commence with your diagnosis. Mania, in fact, only pronounces a predisposition that your acts and thoughts had indicated since you were a child. Manic for the first time in 2007, I tried hard to again reinvent myself as a natty aesthete. The packet of Wills Navy Cut in my pocket was replaced with one of Benson & Hedges. I was sleepless and, with no one to talk to at night, I turned up at a Delhi luxury hotel at two in the morning. With the key to my cramped studio apartment tucked away, I told the receptionist I had just flown in from London. 'My flight was delayed by some six hours. The airline misplaced my luggage. Your hospitality, I know, is the stuff of legend. I have a few hours to wait before my host wakes up. Can you help me make an international call? And if it's not too much to ask, could I bother you for a coffee?'

I mistook the receptionist's courtesy for coquettishness. The hotel's palatial interiors made me assume a Mughal air. I was led to a business centre whose leather tapestry reeked of abundance and the perversion it sanctifies. I made a call to Lucia, my girlfriend in Cornwall. I was meant to move to Britain in July. We were going to get married. June, however, was making our imagined bliss very unlikely. My tone, once mushy, had fast switched to indignant. My sentences were whiplash. I struck where it hurt most. My voice echoed in the chamber as I raged against her.

The malice I felt was only transient. I was given a table at the back of the hotel's coffee shop. 'I thought you'd like one with a sofa, sir. Just so you can put your feet up,' said the receptionist. I took out my diary to scribble a highfalutin note—'Hotels are our last bastion of empathy.' I soon arranged half the contents of my backpack neatly on my table. I placed two notebooks with matching pens on the side. I placed my iPod near the fork and I wore my headphones. Three books

Mistreatment of gf

were placed in front of me and I began reading *Free Love*, a collection of short stories by Ali Smith.

For the next fifteen minutes, I immersed myself in the story 'Text for the Day'. Travelling the world, Melissa tears pages from the books in her library—*Dubliners*, *Madame Bovary*, *Bliss*. She leaves pages of poetry and prose in the oddest of places for strangers to find. A week later, when heading to the airport, I'd litter the streets of Delhi with pages from Virginia Woolf's diary, but that night I furiously copied in my notebook four lines I felt Ali Smith had constructed near perfectly—'There are poems in gutters and drains, under the rails laid for trains, pages of novels on the pavement, in the supermarkets, stuck to people's feet or the wheels of their bikes and cars; there are poems in the desert.' Mania often forces you to map a brave new world. Ali Smith was my ruler.

On a table not very far from mine, a group of four air hostesses were having a late dinner. I looked up to see that the woman who sat at its head was carefully observing my near ritualistic gestures. I stared into her eyes, and she didn't remove her gaze. Convention was beginning to fast lose its hold. We glanced at each other often after that, and before I got up to smoke, I smiled in her direction. I was almost ready to go back inside when I saw her walk into the hotel's open foyer. Urvashi asked if I had a cigarette to spare. Suddenly, I came to inhabit a fantasy. The world was talking back.

Though the air was muggy, Urvashi and I stood outside the hotel's opulent lobby, talking for ten minutes. She told me she lived in Delhi, but had only accompanied her friends here to enjoy a buffet her airline would pick up the tab for. 'Never

has a man had the courage to look me in the eye for so long,'
she said without preamble.

I laughed, and began narrating the story I had earlier
invented for the receptionist. I had moved to England when
I was eighteen. 'I somehow can't seem to study enough. This
PhD will be the death of me.' I told her I was thinking about
coming back to India. 'I just can't have another of my jokes
fall flat. It really does shake my confidence.'   *Urvashi*

Urvashi's parents wanted her to get married, but she
said she wasn't done sowing her wild oats. 'You really are
exceptionally beautiful,' I mumbled with some hesitation. She
smiled and asked if I'd like to meet the day after. 'We both
would have recovered by then,' she said, shaking my hand,
thanking me for the cigarette.

Returning to my table, I felt buoyant. I didn't trust my
phone, so I jotted down Urvashi's number in my notebook.
I couldn't escape the ceremony of the moment. I felt my
fingers acquire a nimble dexterity, and each time I reached
for my cup of coffee, I did so delicately. I played an
imaginary string instrument when listening to my iPod. I
fervently underlined passages in a book. Urvashi was still
my audience, and I overcompensated for my bluff with a
performance. She waved before leaving. I felt relieved.
Finally, I buttered my bread. The text messages we soon
started to exchange were delectably flirtatious, and in just a
few hours, I was convinced I had met the love of my life. 'I
am good with parents,' I typed.

'I could tell,' she replied.

For the third night in a row, I kept myself awake with
cups of coffee that I had given up counting. Around five that

morning, Urvashi called to say goodnight. 'I've never done this before,' she admitted.

'This is the first time for me too. So many things tonight were a first for me,' I said.

She suggested that the next time I get up from my table for a cigarette, I should go stand by the hotel's pool. 'It's great to swim in, but at this time, I think it'll be even better to look at,' she said. I took her advice and went outside to see that the sky was still dark. Lit from the inside, the pool was a shock of blue. The birds which sat on the enclosure's tall trees were waking up. I decided to dip my toes in the water. In what seemed like a single instant, I thought of the Ganges, the Yamuna and the Mansarovar. The ripples I saw were the aftershock of my awakening. The circles of consciousness had found their centre. I wasn't shy of my destiny any more. I was accepting it, one toenail at a time.

While I was sitting in the restaurant, my expansiveness had led me to befriend Giridhar. He had worked in the hotel for nearly two decades and the anecdotes he shared about graveyard shifts, insomnia and Lucknow, his birthplace, were unpretentious and compelling. His stories did not need cultivation. As I sat on a table near the pool, watching the sun rise, Giridhar came out with a tray. He had arranged on it all my belongings and a fresh cup of coffee. He carried my backpack on his shoulder. 'It's a nice morning, sir. I thought you'll enjoy it better out here,' he said.

'It's the first day of the rest of my life,' I said. I tried to disregard the fact that I had started trading in clichés.

Before Giridhar left me to contemplate the sun, he said, 'So many cigarettes are bad for health, sir.'

I smiled and replied, 'I cannot have enough of pleasure, Giridhar.'

The ashtray, placed by the door, was tall and still filled with the remains of half a dozen cigarette butts. My thoughts of Shiva exaggerated my hedonism. Wanting to mirror his form, I dug my hand into the gravel of the tray and smeared its ash all over my forehead. 'You can rub it on, but can you eat it?' I was hearing voices. I licked my palm clean. I told myself I had tasted fire, but as my teeth began to crunch on stone, my annoyance grew. I marched through the hotel's lobby, and in its opulent washroom, I almost bathed at the sink. On my way out, the concierge greeted me. Guests were making their way to the coffee shop. I felt exposed. I was no longer an emperor in disguise. I was one who didn't have clothes on. The comfort of strangers can, perhaps, only be best felt at night.

As I lit another cigarette by the pool, I saw a woman in a bikini, sunbathing on a lounger. Wanting to speak to someone about the perils of desire, needing to feel understood again, I walked up to her. Erica was from Australia. I apologized for invading her privacy. She was awkward. She said she didn't mind. We talked about the weather. I said, 'The only good thing about it is that it affects us all equally.' I admitted to her I had stolen the line from Paul Auster, but she hadn't heard of the American author. I asked her if she felt unsafe in Delhi. 'What was the first thing that ran through your mind when you saw an Indian man walk up to you?' She had just started to reply when I saw the burly hotel manager walking swiftly in my direction. He held me by the arm, lifting me up in one quick motion. The bellboy had picked up my bag and he soon came to grab my other shoulder. The receptionist looked at me with some disdain as I was being thrown out.

'How dare you bother our guests,' the manager shouted in the foyer. 'We've been watching you for a while.' Having picked up my bag, I started walking. I didn't protest. My coffees had all been free.

~

If you wish to live a double life, you have to quickly learn how to separate one from another. I did not tell anyone of my humiliation.

Every woman I met had the potential to be a lover. It hadn't been long since I had quit my job as a journalist at a Delhi newspaper, so my friendships all had a recent history. Memories were still alive enough to be remodelled. I confessed to my former colleagues a desire which I claimed had for long been constant. I played footsie with Aarika, and Ria caressed my cheek after I told her I'd left home.

With acquaintances, I didn't have to invent familiarity. The conversations I had had with Sukriti by our office's coffee machine had always been effortless. I had even helped her move house. When she invited me over to share a bottle of wine, I first acknowledged my expectation. We laughed heartily that night. Every other word she spoke presented me with an opportunity to pun. Jokes were ripe for the picking. The alcohol disguised my lunacy. My candour could easily be dismissed as inebriated levity. Without warning, a garrulous American suitor soon rang the doorbell to interrupt our revelry. The braggart's presence was an imposition. Sukriti tried to apologize for him. His want, though, was more legitimate than mine. His craving was evidently used to satisfaction. I showed myself out. I didn't want to fight.

My head was swimming when I lay on my bed that night. The half bottle of wine had blended with my manic stupor to make sleep possible again. A burning sensation all over my bare back woke me up three hours later. My room was filled with smoke, and as I stood up to see the mattress aflame, I foolishly muttered, 'Dante!' I ran outside, wearing only my boxer shorts. I could see flames leap from a window I had thankfully cracked open. Rather than chastise myself for having stubbed out my cigarette on my bed, I was fascinated by the fire. My pyre had found me, and I had walked through its fire unscathed. I used buckets of water to calm the blaze. My floor was soon covered with ash. I didn't have a bed to sleep on any more.

No conversation starter can ever match the drama of a near-death experience. Fear, pain and misfortune can all be exaggerated to elicit sympathy and wonder. Hearing of my predicaments, a friend offered me her house to stay in. My survival had for long hinged on the kindness of women and I was fast accruing a debt I thought I could repay by only transforming more fully. Walking past a jeweller who advertised his piercings as 'special', I stepped in and asked him to pierce both my ears. Waiting to suffer the hurt of a prick which for me encapsulated women and their vanity, I wanted to learn how to be both. Though the gold studs were ungainly, I felt a childish need to show them off.

Three days after we had first met, Urvashi caught me intently inspecting my reflection in a cafe window when she came in. She was wearing a short skirt with black stockings. 'This is what I wear to work,' she said, perhaps feeling compelled to clarify.

'But you aren't flying today, are you?' My voice already sounded disappointed.

'No, but there's still an office I show my face at sometimes,' she replied, looking pointedly at my earlobes. 'Those are new. You didn't have them the last time.' Bashfulness had suddenly taken the place of my bravado.

'I'd always wanted to get this done, and after that night of firsts, I think I found some strange courage.'

She smiled in a manner I could recognize from the other night. Picking up my pack of cigarettes from the table, she asked why I always flipped the last one.

'I find a new answer to that question each time. I can give you choices.'

She laughed and said, 'I'd like you to invent a line you've never used.'

I must have blushed. 'Because I hope someone will turn my world upside down by the time I count to twenty.' I remember fearing who I was becoming.

I didn't tell Urvashi about the fire. Reality could puncture the lightness of an intimacy we were stitching somewhat briskly. Aware that a Google search would rupture my careful fiction, I made only a few obtuse references to my life in Britain. We talked about how at times she'd feel bloated when she was in the air. I told her I felt bloated all the time.

She told me, 'Beauty is not something I was given. It is something I create every day. It takes me an hour. You can time it.' I told her I was trying to survive without a watch. When she said she was tired of relationships that grew too serious too quickly, I took the hint. I sensed our togetherness was transitory, and though I knew the afternoon came with its limits, I couldn't have felt more content.

'You slowed me down. Thank you for that,' I said, dropping her outside her door. I didn't expect to be called inside, nor did I expect us to be alone. There was no guided tour. She held me by the hand and took me to her room. Before kissing my lips, all Urvashi said was, 'I hope you're counting to twenty.'

For the next hour, we had sex with an abandon that was novel. I again had the attention of my audience, but control was not a prerogative that fully belonged to either one of us. For a brief interlude, I even thought I was free of language. I wanted to communicate my gratitude to Urvashi. Pleasure had always been problematic for me. Surrender was relief. As I buttoned my shirt, she emptied her jewellery box on the bed. She found a silver earring and gave it to me. 'When you take off those studs, put this on. I want to see you wear something that's mine.'

Sadly, sex only interrupted my mania. She and I never met again.

The women I confessed an undying love for were all merely substitutes for one another. I tailored a performance I was soon refining with practice. No bigger than a pocketbook, a collection of Franz Kafka's aphorisms had become a manual for me in that summer of 2007. Three sentences by Kafka illustrated my quandary: 'There are some who assume that next to the original deception, another smaller deception was practiced specifically for them. It's as if when a romantic comedy is performed on stage, the actress, in addition to the lying smile for her beloved, keeps a further, particularly cunning smile for a certain spectator in row Z. That is going too far.' I was the actress, yes, smiling the cunning smile, but I was also the spectator. I was mistaking even the slightest bit of attention for adoration. I'd gone too far.

Pulling me out of his living room, an acquaintance advised, 'Stop thinking you're some kind of Krishna. You're just a really bad actor botching up his once-in-a-lifetime part as Casanova.' I had gotten used to my interactions being bountiful, and was surprised by the ever-increasing possibility of hostility. My utterances had begun to anger those I had once considered my dearest friends. I'd often be irate when talking on the phone. I screamed so loudly when talking to Lucia once, she pleaded from Cornwall, 'Will you please lower your voice? You'll wake Turkey up.' I berated cautious women for leading me up the garden path. Knowing I had become an object of gossip, the conversations I imagined people were having about me were more fact than supposition. When my friend arrived at her door, wanting me to leave that very minute, I assumed the neighbours must have complained. But my transgressions had become hard to dismiss as shenanigans.

Of all the belongings I left behind in my hurry to leave Delhi, I still miss most my library which I had carefully packed in three boxes. Having exhausted all the funds in my bank account and having spent all my favours, I sat in an autorickshaw with nowhere to go. An ex-colleague thankfully brought me some money to pay the hotel I had impulsively checked into. Love makes you think of affection as grace, and you then spend your time trying to match that beneficence. Kanti, my waiter, saw me type on my laptop and asked me how much it would cost to buy one for his teenage son. I made him take mine. To have absolutely nothing, I would have to make use of one last open ticket to Bombay. I left Delhi that night, thinking I was free of attachment.

My childhood friends who I met in Bombay were perturbed enough by my gradual metamorphosis to be more forgiving. Waiting for one of them at the airport, I felt the need to test the limits of my new-found asceticism. I sat cross-legged and began meditating outside the terminal. With no luggage, the Bombay constable found it hard to believe I was a passenger. He shooed me away with his stick. 'This is no place for bums,' he said. My actions were becoming harder to fathom and my misconduct was becoming harder to apologize for. I was making scenes in bars and on the road. It was prudent on the part of my two closest friends to take me to see a psychiatrist. I was fidgety and impatient in the waiting room. The receptionist soon asked me to wait inside. She showed the way.

The room I was led into had three chairs and an examination table. Parvati was filling out forms when I sat down. Her forehead seemed to have locked itself into a frown. She kept removing the hair from her face as she ticked multiple boxes.

I apologized before asking, 'What do they have you in for?'

Her concentration interrupted, she lifted her head and looked like a rabbit that had been caught in the headlights of my question. 'They don't know yet. I don't even know if I should be here.'

I laughed and said that we were in the same boat.

'But looking at you, I think that boat might capsize,' said Parvati.

She was disarmingly attractive when she smiled. When she asked me for my name, I considered the possibilities for a few seconds and said, 'Advaita Goswami.'

'But that's a girl's name, isn't it?' she asked.

My lie had given me the chance to reinvent myself again, and I wanted to cross a threshold I had been too afraid to in the past. 'Advaita literally means non-duality. More simply, it means not two. If I were a Vedanta scholar, I'd tell you there is no gender.'

She asked sheepishly, 'Are you a Vedanta scholar?'

I burst out laughing. I told Parvati I was an orphan, that I had lost my parents in a car accident and that I was now living on an inheritance. I had a sister, but we, for some reason, didn't talk much after our parents' death. 'I know I won't have to worry about money, but I don't know what to do with my freedom.'

She said there was only one way out for me. I needed to get up to mischief. 'But the problem with mischief is that it lands you in trouble, no? I guess that's why I am here.' Before she went back to her forms, I asked her if she'd like to meet for a drink. She tore a piece of paper and wrote down her number. Advaita Goswami was far smoother than Shreevatsa Nevatia could ever be. When the nurse came to get me, thankfully she didn't call out my name.

As I sat across from a psychiatrist for the first time, I leant back and rested my arm on the chair. I was caught in the act. It did not take long.

3

The Invention of Sex

The lies you tell when you are manic are rooted in delusions. When you're inventing fantastic fictions for your audience, you almost forget what truth is. The worlds you conjure exist. You will them to. Speech becomes a ticket to authenticity, and because no fabrication can be impervious to reality, you find your inconsistencies irksome. The guilt, which amplifies itself when you are depressed, is altogether absent when you're becoming someone you had always wanted to be, from an elsewhere you had always wished you inhabited. You lie because your world ought to have been better. The attention and belief of your listener fulfils your wish. Stories are of course undone by outlandish exaggerations, but a manic mind desperately wants to travel distances that have been impossible to cover in moments more prosaic.

Sins, especially those you consider unforgivable, are easier to remember than deeds which were possibly virtuous. The upstanding Rama never lied. Having devoured Ramanand Sagar's televised *Ramayan* when I was four, I grew up believing that dishonesty would consign my soul to a purgatory where

47

I'd be visited by monsters who had talons for nails and tusks for teeth. I never challenged the unreasonable ideal my parents foisted on me. I only internalized it. A plump child, I was never athletic. I was made goalkeeper in the only game of football I ever played. After the ball was kicked straight into my gut, I lay on the field, gasping and winded, and resolved to never play another sport again. It was imperative that all our school's students participate in an annual march-past. I deliberately didn't match my step to the drum. I fell out of line time and again, but was still not asked to return to class. One day, I decided to hold the sides of my belly and scream.

When my class teacher put her hand on my head and asked what was wrong, I said with a wince, 'Appendicitis.' As I told Mrs Sinha that I'd have to be operated on soon, she held my hand and guided me out of the winter sun. I sat on the green benches of our gymnasium and enjoyed the few minutes my warm-hearted teacher fussed over me. She brought me water, gave me a samosa and told me I didn't have to march again that year.

In the days that followed, Mrs Sinha started stopping me in the corridor to ask how I was feeling. She pointed to me once and told a colleague, 'He is only nine.' My fake excuse soon became an elaborate lie. I was racked with guilt, but I realized that an untruth had the power to bring me a lasting affection. When I failed my first maths test, Mrs Sinha told me to meet her after school. She held my face in her hands and asked what was wrong. Not knowing how to shape my experience into narrative, I told her I was finding it hard to concentrate when asked to multiply and divide numbers. I could hardly tell her what the matter really was.

I had always been a talkative child. I would memorize jokes to repeat to my parents' friends and members of my extended family. They would, from time to time, call me over to lighten the mood with my perceived precocity. I never wanted to disappoint the audience of my relatives. More specifically, I never wanted to disappoint Satyah.

For a boy of eight, his eighteen-year-old cousin is often a protector. When I'd fight with friends, standing on a water tank in school, I'd tell them, 'My brother Satyah will come beat you up if you don't shut your mouth.' His newly acquired adulthood and driving licence were, for me, an inexhaustible source of wonder. His aloofness only made him more attractive. Satyah had never taken an interest in my stories or proficiencies, but one day he asked his parents to let me stay over.

I was accustomed to sharing the room with him and his sister, sleeping on the mattress between their two single beds. A deep sleeper since the day I was born, it must have taken Satyah some time to wake me up. 'I have something to show you,' he whispered. I pretended to have a passion for the music he listened to—Roxette, Elton John, Wham! That night I thought he was going to let me see *Top Gun* or *Cocktail*, films that my sister had told me an eight-year-old was too young to watch. He asked me to climb into his bed, and took out from his drawer two magazines, *Debonair* and *Playboy*. 'I'm letting you see these because you have been such a good boy.' As he flipped through their pages, I remember staring with my mouth open. Like most boys my age, the female form repelled and fascinated me. This secretiveness was criminally seductive.

After exhausting *Debonair*, Satyah said, 'This next one is even better.' I looked at blondes and redheads sprawled on chaise longues and the backs of cars. I did not know how to name parts of their anatomy, but Satyah's hands slowly began to roam all over my body. He kept his nails long. He dug them into my skin, dragged them over my chest and nipples, before resting his fingers on my penis. I looked to see the door was unlocked and that my cousin, sleeping on the next bed, was still tossing and turning. The illicitness of my pleasure made me pull off the sheet and return to the mattress. I could hear Satyah laugh. He cautioned, 'If you do tell anyone, they too will laugh at you.'

A few days later, my mother asked me to pack my things for the night. Satyah was coming to pick me up for a sleepover. My reluctance wasn't loud enough and my heart was beating too fast for me to register my protest. Sitting in the passenger seat, I felt afraid; but more troublingly, I also felt shy. He didn't speak for a while, and after ten minutes of him resting his hand on my thigh, he said, 'I have got a video for you today. It's even better than the magazines.' I was not myself that evening. I was letting down my uncle and aunt with a lacklustre performance. When Satyah shook my shoulder that night, I was awake, hysterical with nervousness and anticipation. Taking me to a room which had a television and VCR, he pressed play quickly. The evening's entertainment had already been set up.

I looked at him quizzically when I saw faces that all looked foreign. 'These are my favourite. You call them Oriental. This one is from Japan.' He came and sat next to me on the couch, his arm resting over my shoulders. He said after a pause, 'Have

sexually assaulted

I ever told you you're my favourite brother?' I tried to conceal my excitement with a demure smile. 'I want us to play a game. When I tell you, I want you to do everything to me what the women are doing to the men.' The girls in the video all had bodies like mine, boyish, not quite developed. The men, unrestrained and wanton, seemed to possess a desire that was violent. I grew scared. Suddenly, the fellatio on the TV screen came to be instructive. Satyah picked me up from the sofa and made me kneel before him. He held my hair with his fingers and pushed my head down to his penis. He didn't let go until he had reached orgasm. Terrified, my mouth full of semen that tasted revolting, I looked at the door. This time, it was locked.

Satyah's sudden arrival in my building's foyer became a regular feature. He'd find more excuses to make me stay at his. He would take me into the shower with him and make me trim his pubic hair. He would reach for my hand when no one was looking and leave it pressed between his legs. I hid my bruises well. When I told him that my dry orgasms hurt the most, he said, 'You just need to wait a little. You'll be a bigger boy. I know I am waiting for that.' Satyah had started fondling my pudgy body as if it were a woman's. One night, he pointed to a painting of Saraswati that hung in his room. The artist had endowed the body of the goddess with a curvaceous fullness, and my cousin pointed to her breasts and said, 'When I look at her in the mornings, I only think of you. I just cannot help it.'

The guilt I felt soon after can only be described as Oedipal. Mothers are not meant to be desired, and craving a goddess was certainly a crime that deserved an even greater punishment. I had been included in a triangle of lust that was too depraved to merit forgiveness. I was surrounded by images of deities at home and in Calcutta's streets. In the benevolent eyes of gods, I saw an anger that no penance could ever placate. Begging for mercy, I started saying fervent and silent prayers I knew would go unanswered. For half an hour before the school's first bell rang, I would kneel in its chapel, pleading for absolution. I was the sinner, not Satyah. My guilt had transformed into shame because God was always looking. I would kiss the feet of Jesus and drink the holy water, but I was regrettably never Christian enough for confession.

Distress becomes tolerable when it is predictable. Sitting in the passenger seat of Satyah's car had become habit, and because I didn't need to be instructed any more, once-forbidden rituals had begun to seem mechanical. For a few minutes, I would intently listen to the stereo play Hindu bhajans that inspired in Satyah a strange rapture. My eyes would look out for the white marble of the Victoria Memorial. On the dome of this palatial monument stands the Angel of Victory, a conspicuous black statuette, who can be seen blowing a bugle. Traffic thinned when she appeared, and, as if on cue, Satyah would unzip his pants and reveal his half-erect penis. My right hand knew exactly how he liked it stroked. I had stopped worrying about truckers being able to watch my fingers glisten with a fluid that signalled an imminent ejaculation. Seclusion, I knew, would soon be found. Satyah made sure of it. He would park his car under trees or near open fields, turn off the car's ignition, and I'd learnt when to crouch in my seat. My tongue was adept at teasing his arousal.

If the sun was still out when Satyah came to pick me up, I'd know his desire had turned desperate. Secrets are better shared at night. It was approximately nine one night when he stopped his car on the periphery of Calcutta's racecourse. I had my head between his legs and had almost started to taste the relief of his climax when I heard a loud rap on the car window. Looking up, my lips dripping with his cum, I saw the uniform of a police officer. The smile on his lips was typically fiendish. Satyah rubbed my face with a damp cloth he used to wipe his windscreen, and then rolled down his window. The inspector demanded that we both step out of the car. Tears had started rolling down my cheeks and I was begging the officer to let us go. Holding his dark glasses in one hand and Satyah's with another, he looked at me and said with a raised voice, *'Chup kor, rendi shaala!'* ('Shut up, you fucking prostitute!') The state had intervened, but at ten, I had little idea my solicitousness could be monetized. I was good at doing what Satyah had me do and I felt my crime was my skilfulness.

Julie Andrews would come to me when I found myself in times of trouble. Addicted to *The Sound of Music*, envious of a childhood that afforded pranks and impromptu songs, as an eight-year-old, I saw the film twenty-three times in a month. Maria, whose disposition I would try hard to emulate, had taught me to think of my favourite things when I was feeling sad. Refusing to move, I sat inside. Seeing Satyah stand with his head lowered and the police officer looking increasingly irate, I thought about burying my face in my grandmother's cupboard, smelling her eau de cologne, the starch of her sarees and her tobacco. I cried more inconsolably then, thinking I was going to be put away. Half an hour later, Satyah came to take my watch, a gift from my grandfather on my birthday. They had taken his watch and wallet too. 'I'll kill you if you tell anyone about this,' Satyah said after taking the steering wheel again. He had never threatened me before and as I continued sobbing, more quietly now, he drove at breakneck speed. With my hands failing to grab the dashboard, I pleaded with him to slow down. If he had been booked for speeding, though, the night would have perhaps been more comical than terrifying.

The drives didn't stop. They just became more perilous. I'd look at the speedometer and usually see that we were travelling at over a hundred kilometres an hour. He started pulling on my hair when he made my head go down on his penis. On the nights I stayed at his house, he would part my buttocks with a ferocity I had not known. I'd return home with scratches on my hands and sides. My grandmother always assumed my sister was to blame, and I'd take pleasure in seeing her scolded. She'd only scratch me more after and unknowingly make my alibi more credible. When a dermatologist examined the swelling of my inner thighs, he asked me to lose weight. 'Your thighs rub against one other. You have rashes because you're fat,' he said. I felt embarrassed, yet relieved.

Rather used to women tugging at my chubby cheeks, I had never considered my corpulence a detriment. My extended family was large. For my nine cousins to all fit at a table, we needed ten chairs. Our visit to Calcutta's newest bakery had left me excited. When asked what I'd like to eat, I pointed to two stuffed buns that looked the most drenched in cheese. I must have been biting into my bread with some relish when Satyah shouted from the other end of the table, 'Put that down this very minute! Have you looked at yourself in the mirror? You're obese enough to break the chair you're sitting on. You're not even a girl and you have bigger breasts than the woman behind the counter.' I looked around to see that the cashier was particularly well endowed. I was too startled to cry. Thankfully, Satyah stormed out of the cafe.

My torment would lift me up with pleasure and then punish me by throwing me straight down with a painful blow. A sizeable crop of recent studies in the West have concluded that childhood trauma makes victims of sexual abuse more susceptible to the swings of bipolarity. A research paper published in the January 2016 edition of the *International Journal of Bipolar Disorders* reads, 'Childhood trauma leads to alterations of affect regulation, impulse control, and cognitive functioning that might decrease the ability to cope with later stressors.' Talking about consequences that are 'pathophysiological', such findings have a tendency to make the relation between abuse and bipolarity a causal one. Though I feel tempted to agree with authors and psychiatrists who, for instance, render my drug dependency a direct outcome of my sexual initiation, I do still feel the need to atone for my lapses. Manic depression is a whodunnit, and the suspects are often many—genetic predisposition, chemical imbalances in the brain, environmental factors. I have never blamed Satyah for my affliction, but trapped between his depravity and my humiliation, I discovered an oscillation I'd recognize when I'd be manic and on see-saws again.

In 2007, days after I had been diagnosed as bipolar, a counsellor asked me if I had ever been depressed. I was quick to answer, 'No,' but my mother would remember a different history. When I was in class six, I had stopped talking at home altogether. A painting in my neighbour's living room had taught me that pensiveness was most keenly felt when looking out of the window, a palm cupping your chin, your eyes centred on a distant somewhere. It helped that we lived on the thirteenth floor of a high-rise. By the time I was eleven, I wasn't left with many friends. The company of more carefree classmates made me feel clumsy, obese and reprehensible. When I refused the third birthday invitation, my mother decided to intervene. She drove up to school and asked my class teacher, 'Have you seen any change in Shreevatsa lately?' Beverly Fernandes called me an introvert, adding that I never played with the other boys. My mother pleaded with her, asking her to somehow include me more. So the next day, Ms Fernandes walked into class to announce that I was the new assistant monitor. Though discipline had never exactly been a forte, a teacher had again cured my grief with kindness.

My sister had encouraged me to keep a diary. 'It'll help with your English, idiot,' she said, while smacking my head. I looked for a notebook that was pretty, and the only empty one I could find had a picture of the incorruptible Rama on its cover. All my entries, as a result, were reverential and meek. In a manner that I would pompously refer to as Proustian later, I described in some detail the Christian infidelities of my Hindu soul, the junk food my grandmother would spoil me with and the comeliness of Ms Fernandes's new kurta. I had of course devoured my sister's diary and I was worried she would nose her way into mine. I had to be discreet. It took me a few months to disregard the possibility of discovery.

In an entry dated 7 December 1994, I bravely tried to explain the difference between good and bad. My grandfather was easy to idolize. When he returned home from the club, spent after three hours of gin and bridge, he would sit in a corner unobtrusively. I would sit next to him, listening to the day's gossip our family revelled in. His attentiveness was only half-hearted.

He would walk up the steps of his home, holding my hand, asking me about school and my last report card. When upstairs, he would sometimes reach for his wallet and give me a hundred-rupee note. I'd instinctively know that the winnings that night had been considerable. 'I want to be like my grandfather,' I told that dear diary. 'I want to drink his whisky. I want to spend all my nights in his room.' When I went to live with my grandfather, he let me play Tetris till the wee hours of the morning. He found joy in disobeying my mother's edicts. 'She is my daughter,' he once told me. 'She listens to me. I don't listen to her.'

Satyah's defiance, in comparison, was not as quiet or kind. I had grown used to lying on his mattress, pretending to be asleep. I knew the hour he would come to wake me up. It had taken me three years before I would write I was finally bored of sex. 'I don't want to do bad things. My knees are scraped. How will I kneel in the chapel? I am so sorry. Please help me,' I wrote.

Despite me leaving my Ramayana diary in places where it could easily be found—on top of our writing desk, under the toilet sink, next to her Sweet Valley High—my sister's curiosity was never piqued. She and I had substituted the intensity of our fights for the pleasures that satellite television offered. The journal Doogie Howser MD kept on his computer helped us think that compared to the adolescence of a boy genius who saved lives, fell in love and let his best friend in through his window, our teenage years were comfortably fluffy, even if more mundane. We couldn't get enough of the misunderstandings that made *Beverly Hills, 90210* so compelling, and after watching *The Wonder Years*, I began fancying myself as the dorky Kevin Arnold. Our neighbour, I imagined, was a Winnie Cooper lookalike and each time I saw her, I put my hands in my pockets and looked sheepish.

Of all the television my sister and I devoured, I liked *Baywatch* the most. Though my sister was four years older and didn't let me read her Mills and Boon, she found red swimsuits permissible. The lithe female form of the show's lifeguards was alluring, not pornographically gauche. The poster I put up in our room had David Hasselhoff with a buxom co-star on each arm. My sister looked at it and said, 'You do know he is gay, right?' When she saw me look perplexed, she asked me to bring the heavy Webster's dictionary our father kept in the living room. I looked for 'gay' and read, 'Happy and excited; cheerful and lively.' She laughed and pointed to the second meaning, 'Of, relating to, or used by homosexuals.' I was still puzzled. I looked up 'homosexual' and said out loud, 'Of, relating to, or involving sexual intercourse between persons of the same sex.' For days after, I would think of the distaste in my sister's voice when she had said 'gay'.

When I was twelve, I grew obsessed with the word 'homosexual', and poring over the tomes in my parents' library, desperate for a clue, I learnt an essential lesson which expedited research in my college and journalistic years:

Comfort in television.

sexuality

always try starting with books that come with an index. The nineteen leather-bound volumes of Encyclopaedia Britannica didn't have a single reference to homosexuality, so I naturally concluded that history didn't care. Religion, however, did. Libraries of Jesuit schools expectedly stock various editions of the Bible, and ours had on a dedicated shelf at least eight versions—King James, the Good News Bible and half a dozen standard translations. I knew these books well, and had, in the past, taken a couple home. I was thirteen when I saw during recess, a fatter Bible in the 'New Arrivals' section. The blue jacket had a cross that was etched in gold. Seeing me marvel at the binding, Albert Singh, our genial but sometimes crotchety librarian, told me, 'This has the Old and the New Testament in one volume. You can't borrow it, but read it here if you want to.'

I was alone in the reading room that afternoon. The first thing I did was look under 'H' for 'homosexual', and I found six page numbers listed. Though I expected damnation, I was also hopeful I would find a prescription for redemption. Thinking it best to start with the Old Testament, I turned to the eighteenth chapter of Leviticus, and read to myself its twenty-second verse: 'You shall not lie with a male as with a woman; it is an abomination.' My heart sank. This was certainly not a good start. I foolishly convinced myself that the thirteenth verse of Leviticus's twentieth chapter would be gentler. 'If a man lies with a male as with a woman, both of them have committed an abomination; they shall surely be put to death; their blood is upon them.' All I needed now was a crucifix. The New Testament only worsened my anxiety. I would receive a recompense that fit my 'shameful' error. The chapel seemed hostile after that day. I had angered Jesus, but worse still, I felt I had lost the affection of Mary.

Studying feminism, some seventeen years later, I would again come to feel ashamed, this time of my heterosexuality. The tumult that resulted from my sexual initiation had made me wary of masculinity and its many manifestations. 'I feel guilty being a man,' I said in a gender studies class one day.

My lecturer's question was deft: 'Are you saying that you feel guilty for the sins patriarchy has committed or that you'd much rather be a woman?'

I was being cocky when I replied, 'There must be a way to be both.'

In *Persuasion*, Jane Austen writes, 'When pain is over, the remembrance of it often becomes a pleasure.' Pain, for me, had strangely become the remembrance of pleasure. There was a thrill in being a surrogate woman, but despite several attempts, I could never again muster an ounce of sexual desire for men. My complexity gave me an intellectual swagger, and I found something comic in the tragedy I mourned. Rather than rely on vague allusions, I could directly address my hurt. I'd never need to write my stories of sex and sexuality in shorthand again.

Adolescence brought with it a rare agency. Not only could I protest staying at Satyah's, I could also refuse to go with him for a drive in his car. On the few occasions that I did succumb to both his and my appetites, I lost interest in a matter of minutes. I'd think of the death that the Bible had promised or, only to annoy him, I'd start humming a Backstreet Boys or Spice Girls tune. Satyah himself had turned more circumspect and had begun to trim his nails regularly. Respite did not come with an announcement. Four years after he woke me up in the middle of the night, my cousin would now let me sleep. Suddenly, I could read again. Language became a cure, and I was less fearful of biblical retribution.

A few months later, the excitement in my mother's voice was audible when she asked my sister and me to wear our best. 'Satyah is engaged.' As the family—my nine cousins and their parents—came together in a house I had cryptically described to a friend as the 'den of vice', I felt an inexplicable need to sulk. My moping was only exacerbated when I was told that Satyah had taken his fiancée for a drive. The envy I felt, territorial and consuming, then seemed mysterious, but when I remember my gripe now—'But he kissed me first'—it seems clear I was a boy in love. It only took a jibe from my sister for me to sob in the car that night: 'Boys don't cry.'

On the day Satyah got married, I wore the forlorn expression of a former girlfriend who had been invited to her lover's wedding. My family had always presumed he and I were close, so it was only natural that they pushed me to sit by his side while he jumped through the day's many ceremonial hoops. Even at fourteen, I detected a brutal irony in the pictures of Satyah flanked by his bride and me.

My grandmother did not believe in censorship. She didn't cover my eyes when Julie Andrews kissed Christopher Plummer. I was allowed to watch with her a TV serial that used as its narrative pivot the infidelity of its protagonist. She didn't ask me to change the channel when I started playing *Bandit Queen*. One afternoon, I came back from school to find her watching *The Priya Tendulkar Show*. I knew Priya Tendulkar as a firebrand. She was Rajani, the activist housewife who corrected society from her kitchen. As a chat-show host, she again seemed to have betterment on her mind. The face of the boy she was interviewing that day had been blurred. He started speaking to her about how his uncle would molest him behind closed doors. I was uncomfortable. The secret this nameless teenager was so painfully disclosing felt stolen. Tendulkar kept repeating, 'Here is a victim of sexual abuse.'

The term 'abuse' immediately offered a consolation. The anguish of my private experience could now be explained publicly. 'Abuse' itself suggested a narrative I would not have to detail. My mind, which by then had flagellated itself to the point of exhaustion, breathed a sigh of relief. Participation in an act, pleasurable and painful, did not amount to volition. Though guilt still festered, I didn't feel entirely responsible. 'Victim', on the other hand, caused me to first pity myself. Under warm blankets and hot showers, I started admonishing a world that had wronged me. My adolescence came to be subsumed by a single, stubborn question—'Why me?' You might not have a choice while being victimized, but victimhood, I learnt, is almost always only an alternative. Rather than attributing nurture, concern and warmth to grace, I considered them entitlements. I may never have voiced my demands, but insidious want, I knew well, is more treacherous than those obviously explicit. When called a 'survivor' for the first time, I said, 'My survival has a life of its own. I wish I did too.' I wanted my sister to smack me on the head.

Though I was once told the psyche is best healed by forgiveness, my own few attempts in the past twenty years have unfortunately failed dramatically. I have shaken Satyah's hand, given him tight hugs, talked about the weather and the latest Hollywood release, but the sanctimonious pleasure I have received from these moments of largesse has never quite matched the delight of plotting my revenge.

I imagine Satyah paralysed, mute and bedridden. He will be living alone in a house when I suddenly move in with only one backpack. I would relieve the domestic help of all his duties and become the greying Satyah's primary caregiver. I'd make sure I'd keep the house spotless and on a stereo I'd play a tape I'd recorded. As I'd change his diapers, feed him dinner and give him sponge baths, my cousin would hear a detailed account of how and where he had touched my body as a child. I'd describe to him how limp his body looked now and then remind him of all the stamina that defined his youth. The tape would play on loop for days on end, and then finally, weeks later, as I'd get bored of my ruthlessness, I'd tie a rope from the ceiling of his room and, as he looked on, I'd hang myself. The stereo would only stop when the electric company cut the supply for unpaid bills.

The malice of my imagination and its exaggerated morbidity are excesses I use to level the playing field. When manic, my mind always returns to Satyah's original sin, and this act of revenge is the only vision of justice I consider retributive enough. My actions themselves, though, are far more timid.

In February 2016, disappointed by the fact that I had never confronted my oppressor, I called Satyah at half seven in the morning. His wife picked up and then passed him the phone. 'Do you remember what you did to me as a child?' I was growling, but he was incredulous. I repeated my question, only this time I stressed the word 'child'.

He sounded meek when he mumbled, 'Yes.'

I said, 'I remember only too well all that you did, and in the event that you've forgotten any of it, I'd have no trouble refreshing your memory.'

After a deliberate silence, he asked, 'Why are you telling me this?'

In a voice I tried to lower, I replied, 'Because you need to know I was fragile and am still picking up the pieces. Please don't do this to anyone else.'

I was emboldened by my mania, but I didn't have the heart to scratch the wound I had inflicted. Two decades later, I was still a boy in love.

4

Difficult Loves

Freud had me convinced that no matter how old I grew, I would always only be a child. A counsellor, in her effort to revise the datedness of my thinking, told me, 'Freud is so old-fashioned. Reading him will only make you romanticize the tragedies of your past. You're thirty, not eight.' I didn't have the courage or the patience to demur. My mind was prone to disaster and it was only in Freud that I found a map which helped me understand its troubled geography. In several hour-long sessions with my Freudian psychoanalyst, I had thankfully been encouraged to talk about the anguish of my childhood, and while that dialogue considerably helped cure my torment, it also revealed to me patterns of my behaviour. Satyah's moods would oscillate like a metronome, and as a result, I'd teeter between gratification and fear. The curve of my mania would come to mirror this pendulum of feeling, but each time I fell in love, I'd ride that same roller coaster.

When she first entered a Bombay studio apartment I lived in, a lover exclaimed, 'It is scary how neat this place is.' Her surprise wasn't without cause. My bed sheet had been smoothed right down to the edges. The angles my duvet made were perpendicular. My books were immaculately piled, and all the dishes had been returned to their place after they had dried. Having recently met Gauri at a press briefing, I had told her I was bipolar when I lit her first cigarette. I was not trying to impress her. In the weeks to follow, she would come to learn that my compulsiveness disguised a quiet turbulence. I cleaned the way I loved. Even the tiniest specks of disappointment and acrimony had to be wiped away with an alacrity I otherwise reserved for the stains on coffee cups. I liked emotions the way I liked my furniture, symmetrical, aligned. If Gauri looked peeved, if she sounded impatient, the effects of her mood on mine would be catastrophic. Her affection placed me at the centre of the world, and even the more transient of her frustrations threatened to bring on its end. Much like in my housekeeping, I could not bear the untidiness of anger, fights or recrimination. The problem was, rancour often spilt out.

In his book *The Course of Love*, author Alain de Botton explains the predicament of anxious lovers in terms that sound clinically precise. He writes, 'A sign of an anxiously attached person is an intolerance of, and dramatic reaction to, ambiguous situations—like a silence, a delay or a non-committal remark. These are quickly interpreted in negative ways, as insults or malevolent attacks.' Sitting by my phone, checking it every few minutes, waiting for Gauri to call or text, feeling despondent when she had not, my anxiety fit the pitiable traits of de Botton's description. Loving Gauri taught me that I was not just a slave to attention, I also craved constant affirmation. To survive, love needed to be declared, and to flourish, togetherness needed a flurry of WhatsApp messages.

Tired of being a rare accommodation in her busy schedule, I once told Gauri, 'I hate it when you take your love away.'

Unflustered by my crude sentimentality, she said, 'Only I go away, not my love.' Ever since I was a child, I had been vulnerable to sweetness.

I needed therapy to survive the assault of my anxieties. My psychoanalyst asked, 'Has it ever occurred to you that love relationships can never bring you the plenitude you seek?' I had never considered the possibility that nostalgia was more pernicious than bipolarity. 'Your girlfriends cannot and should not be your grandmother, nor are they stand-ins for Satyah.' Unconditional love is a utopia inhabited by lovers who are young and often unmarried. It is a lie they repeat with mush in their voices and with faces that are kept straight.

Only grandparents, I believe, removed as they are from direct responsibility, have the capacity to love without expectation. My grandmother never concerned herself with my grades or the weight her buttery potatoes had made me gain. Her affection hinged on her indulgence.

My psychoanalyst once asked me, 'You do understand, right, that this love is improbable because it failed to acknowledge reality?'

My paradise felt lost. 'She is dead,' I said. 'I do tend to forget that.'

In her tribute to Freud, the poet Hilda Doolittle had written that 'we are all haunted houses'. I exorcised the ghost of my grandmother fairly quickly, but the spectre of Satyah continued to terrorize me. He had made me eager to please, and my ceaseless supply of tenderness did come with its set of unreasonable demands. Four years of being picked up and dropped by Satyah had left me frightened of rejection. I never grew accustomed to the indifference that followed his orgasms or the disdain on his face when we met at a family lunch. I expected from Gauri an assiduity and warmth that was uninterrupted. I would think the worst if she fell silent for a day. My deficiencies, I'd think, were discernible. In my mind, we had broken up a dozen times.

We were sitting by the window of a Bombay flat, trying to look at the sea in the faint light of the moon, when Gauri said she had something to tell me. 'You need to find for yourself a life of your own, one that doesn't include me.'

After my initial paranoia, I grew resentful and asked, 'So, you're basically asking me to get a life?'

Gauri remained calm. 'I've learnt that you're only setting yourself up for disappointment when you make someone else your only source of fulfilment.'

As we sat in a rickshaw that evening, I felt my indignation give way to reason. I had put too many of my eggs in her basket, and their weight was proving too heavy. In the weeks that followed, Gauri grabbed me by the scruff of my neck each time she saw me sulk. I still felt like a child of eight at times, but I was soon able to whisper in Gauri's ear, 'I am not scared.'

Impressionable minds are corrupted by art, and mine only supports that warning. A good love story in a book or a film has never only been relished. I have felt I had to emulate it or at least use it as a measure of the distance my relationships had the legs to cross. Sadly, I have always been a sappy romantic. I was sixteen, discovering the joys of a faraway literature, when I chanced upon *Difficult Loves*, a collection of short stories by Italo Calvino. It took Calvino just four pages to change my life.

Arturo Massolari, protagonist of 'The Adventure of the Married Couple', works the night shift. He comes home at seven, and the sound of his footsteps and the alarm clock merge in the mind of Elide, his wife. She meets him in the kitchen, 'always such a mess, her face half-asleep'. If Arturo brings her coffee in bed, they embrace. Elide needs to rush to work. Half-naked, they shove each other by the sink. When scrubbing each other's back, they let a caress slip in. He listens for the shriek of the tram to know she has boarded it, then gets into bed and lies on his half. Slowly, he stretches over to Elide's side, into her 'niche of warmth'. Waiting for Elide to return, Arturo soaks the laundry and sweeps a little. They get on each other's nerves when she comes home, but then can hardly eat in their longing to hold hands. It is now time for Arturo to leave. Elide gets into bed, and 'from her own half, lying there, she would slide one foot towards her husband's place, looking for his warmth, but each time she realized it was warmer where she slept, a sign that Arturo had slept there too, and she would feel a great tenderness'. Calvino had described an intimacy I'd always thought ineffable.

Years later, I would excitedly call Gauri and say, 'I've found it. I've found our story.' An education in literary theory had taught me how to join the dots that didn't always belong on the same page. Gauri would send me lunch in the office, and I'd wash her thermos while waiting for her to return home. She'd surprise me with a shirt she'd bought on a whim on her way back and I'd hide toe rings in places I knew she'd look. When brushing our teeth, we'd try and monopolize the bathroom mirror. Our time together, circumscribed as it was, could be measured by counting the cups of coffee I'd drink.

Like Arturo and Elide, we'd quarrel sometimes. She'd be preoccupied and I'd be greedy for primacy when her mind travelled. Our yearning would often get the better of us and we'd hug for minutes together. I'd wake up to see a strand of hair on her pillow. I'd bury my face there, wanting to savour her smell and a little more sleep. Gauri and I had spoilt each other too much. We never did want to get married, but our adventure, I told her on the phone, matched Calvino's perfectly. I was using literature to idealize our togetherness, and Gauri was indulgent. Adaptation, she knew, had fewer side effects than lithium.

There is undoubtedly something self-serving about using literary and cinematic narratives to map—somewhat obsessively—the progression of one's life. Gauri saw this. But my bipolarity, she also believed, absolved my narcissism. Mania deludes me into believing my memory is eidetic, while medication and depression can sometimes give rise to an amnesia that seems permanent. The pickle jars of literature and film have proved to be reliable preservatives. I have fun when crossing my stars with those of fiction. There is no consequence, and very little fault. Films are easy loot. They can be watched again and again. I've found that the lines actors repeat can effortlessly align themselves with parallels I draw. Their stories have allowed me to plot my own graph. Even gestures, I'd say, tell a tale that's mine. When I find it hard to recollect moments of levity, films facilitate recall and escape.

In magazines and newspapers, a signature motif has come to define modern illustrations of mental health afflictions. The manic-depressive mind, in particular, is often depicted as a secluded prison. As a result, these visual representations all unwittingly say that if you are bipolar, your chances of freedom are slim. There is admittedly something a tad nauseating about the suggestion that love can unlock those dark cells. But in my experience, love is more of a break-in, a stealthy rescue mission. Maudlin as it undoubtedly sounds, I have been saved by love a few times over, and each time, I have expectedly found precedents for my liberation in films. Three films in particular—*Apur Sansar* (1959), *Eternal Sunshine of the Spotless Mind* (2004), *Garden State* (2004)— have stencilled my affections. They have helped me come of age, and even made me a better lover.

Home *is* the world

Not yet eighteen, I was standing in the prompt box of a half-darkened theatre when a friend came up to me with a chicken sandwich. I'd never tasted meat before, and right after I had taken that first forbidden bite, I declared dramatically, 'I am going to try everything in the world at least once, and I will watch every Satyajit Ray film at least twice.'

My grandmother assisted me in my transgressions. She never told my parents that I had sneakily started smoking cigarettes, hanging out of my bedroom window. She also gave me money to buy copies of Ray films she'd sit by my side to watch. We giggled uncontrollably during *Sonar Kella*. We relished *Charulata* and *Nayak*, sitting in our respective corners of her bed, but it was the Apu trilogy which really proved moving. In *Pather Panchali* and *Aparajito*, Ray had punctured bleakness with an optimism my grandmother fast started to advocate. 'Be like Apu,' she told me, egging me on to follow the heart. As a result, I was already predisposed to empathy when pushing *Apur Sansar* (*The World of Apu*) in our CD tray.

While it is hard for me to count just how many times I have watched the last film of Ray's trilogy over the years, I do now know the exact progression of Ravi Shankar's score. I feel I can say this with some surety—I know Apu intimately. I know how he thinks. The film opens with Apu visiting the house of a former professor. He needs a letter of recommendation. Claiming to have spotted his talent, the genial and reassuring lecturer encourages Apu to continue writing. Apu's bashfulness became a model that helped me better respond to the few compliments I'd receive for my amateurish writing while I was still in school. The nervousness of his laugh schooled me in diffidence.

Underpaid and often undervalued, journalists have a tendency to look at themselves as impoverished. My imagined pains did not compare to Apu's hardships—he had to pawn his books to pay rent—but like him, I kept buying cigarettes I could ill afford. Our rooms were equally spartan. A picture of Tagore hung on his wall and I had made a photograph of Gabriel García Márquez my computer's wallpaper. Apu didn't want a day job. He said Dickens, Keats, Lawrence and Dostoevsky didn't need one. When I quit my position at a newspaper, I had a similar set of heroes in whose footsteps I wanted to follow—J.M. Coetzee, Raymond Carver, Albert Camus and Italo Calvino. We both were writing novels that were autobiographical, and even though my actions were never significant, Apu taught me how to not be defeated.

When I gave a friend an early draft of my book's first chapters, I wanted him to be astonished, just as Pulu was after reading Apu's manuscript, sitting beside him on a boat. I had always taken my grandmother seriously. I couldn't be any more like Apu.

For the first half hour of *Apur Sansar*, Apu never encounters a woman. Pulu then takes him along to attend the wedding of his cousin, and it is only when the bride's mother sees Apu that we can gauge his desirability. 'I have seen you before,' she tells him. 'You look just like the Krishna I worship.' I have yearned to hear these exact words each time my mind turns manic. Unlike me, though, Apu does nothing to perpetuate this comparison. As the hour of the wedding comes around, we find him sleeping under a tree, unknowingly consecrating the flute he holds. Pulu wakes him up. Tragedy, he says, has befallen his family. The groom, it turns out, is mad. The wedding has been called off, but if Aparna, his cousin, doesn't get married within a few hours, she will forever be cursed. Apu needs to marry her and save the day. A rational and literate writer, Apu is offended by the demands of superstition. He hasn't even shaved.

Apu has never met Aparna. When he changes his mind, he is not driven by compassion. He agrees to marry a woman he doesn't know because he wants to do something great, monumental, something literary. In a shot that Ray frames perfectly, we see Apu and the mad groom, Binu, cross paths. I have stopped at this scene many times and have found in it a metaphor that explains perfectly my experiences of love, its hopes and discontents. My madness has made several of my relationships untenable. Time and again, I have crumbled under the pressure of togetherness and expectation. As I start to break down, I break up, and the altar, once imagined meticulously while lying in bed on lazy Sunday afternoons, becomes an impossible destination. I have often been the Binu who comes to his wedding, wanting a happily ever after, only to be carried away in his finery. Binu's departure, however, allows me to channel my Apu without interruption. Before our leaps of faith, he and I are scared and reluctant, but we're equally desirous of grandeur.

On his wedding night, the only intimacy an honourable Apu delights in is that of confession. Aparna knows he is a writer. He looks discernibly gleeful when she adds, 'I know you write well.' She knows he is an orphan, but as Apu discovers, she doesn't know he is penniless. Apu might have been impervious to his poverty when he tried living reclusively, but he had never fetishized it. The prospect that his lack will now be shared makes him detail his adversities for the first time. 'Will you be able to suffer with me too?' His question is marked by an anticipation that is almost desperate. Her reply—'Why would I not?'—first brings relief, and then, suddenly, Apu laughs ecstatically. I learnt then that the participation of another sometimes affords even more comfort than alleviation.

Dating apps invariably force one to play games of capricious roulette. But the one Kritika and I had signed up on said it prized compatibility over thrills or geographical proximity. She was in Delhi, and I was in Calcutta. We were both journalists. We both liked to read, and as the first flurry of our messages made clear, we were both pernickety about our grammar. For the first week, when we described to each

other the order of our days and thoughts, language facilitated
an affinity that was unencumbered by any scepticism. Asking
for her number, I felt audacious, and three days after we had
grown accustomed to the other's voice, I thought an honest
disclosure would only be ethical. I timidly admitted to Kritika
I was bipolar. As I described to her the peril of my mood
swings, the side effects of my medication and the agony of
my internments, all I was really asking was this—'Will you
be able to suffer with me too?' Kritika was reassuring. 'You're
so brave. Honey, I'm in for the penny. I'm in for the pound.'

She kicked me when I snored. She took me to church on
Christmas, and after I had pleaded with her, Kritika watched
Apur Sansar a second time. Ray, she pointed out, takes just
fifteen minutes to convey a sense of the wholesome bliss that
Apu and Aparna find in a marriage we quickly forget was
accidental. At one point, Apu unexpectedly begins to sulk.
Seeing Aparna break coal to fire the stove, he imagines his
financial insufficiencies have left his young wife filled with
regret. She could have found a richer husband. In a moment
that could soothe the lingering boyhood of any grown man,
Aparna scolds him softly and asks him to stop being a child.
Kritika took to admonishing me with a similar tenderness
as we sent each other stills from the film. *Apur Sansar* soon
became the script we followed when performing our piece of
love. My honesty, though, came with its limits. I didn't tell
Kritika that while I was trying to lessen the distance between
us by enacting the affections I had memorized, *Apur Sansar*
also made me think of Ira and Kamya, two lovers I had
earlier moved in with. I didn't know marriage, but I knew the
pleasures of intimacy cohabitation brings.

Directly translated from Bengali, *sansar* does mean 'world', but mothers in Calcutta—especially those who tie their keys to the end of their sarees—often employ the word when goading their daughters to be more domestic. 'Sansar' comes to include the wily grocer, the errant help and the roguish electrician. When matters of the world are discussed, the matters of home must come first. The householder, ordinary wisdom dictates, is the most worldly of us all. Though solitude comes with its set of sorrows, it also inspires nonchalance. With no one to judge our shabbiness, we can spill ink on our bed sheets and leave the lights on in the morning. The mere presence of a lover brings home the gaze of that 'sansar'. We start shaving a little more frequently. We try and tuck in that paunch. We buy a vacuum cleaner. Apu's transition is similar, but Ray relies on props to capture his metamorphosis. His home soon becomes a museum of affection.

Objects always mattered to Ray, but the curtain that hangs in Apu's room is, for him, an obsession. Torn, a huge hole gaping in its middle, the rag is not just a sign of abjection. It is also a marker of Apu's bachelorhood. He need not care because he has nothing to hide or protect. Aparna feels overwhelmed when she enters Apu's ramshackle room for the first time, and it is through that gash in the burlap that we see her cry. But then, in the matter of a minute, we are taken to the window again, only this time, it has a real floral curtain, the kind that flutters gingerly in the wind. Time, we guess, has been kind, and the contours of Apu's new abundance have quite obviously been defined by Aparna's femininity. I couldn't help but think of *Apur Sansar* when Kamya broke off a kiss to look around our unfurnished home and say,

'We really do need new curtains.' The room I had signed a lease agreement for was no bigger than Apu's, and like his tenement, our Delhi *barsati* also came with a terrace. I had mapped far too many parallels already.

Domesticity, I had always believed, needs to be participative for it to be joyous. Working for a newsmagazine, my hours were too erratic for me to help Kamya peel potatoes and dice the chicken. She said she found a therapeutic delight in cooking us dinner. Every day I'd return home to find that she had factored in my obstinate fussiness when sweating it out with a pressure cooker and a spatula. Apu and Aparna would take turns to fan each other while they ate, but my feminist conscience found little relief in just doing the dishes. The inequities of our labour left me crippled with guilt. I began insisting we eat out more, and on the days we didn't, I found work to keep me in the office for an extra hour or two. *Apur Sansar* was not the narrative we aped. We devoured banal television instead. Though I had always held that compatibility is inessential, I was comforted by the interests Kamya and I shared—Quentin Tarantino, Kishore Kumar, Baudrillard. We hardly ever discussed the fragility of reality, though. Even our conversations about the weather proved dishearteningly matter-of-fact.

When I decided to move in with Kamya, I was watchful. My *Apur Sansar* dream had already soured once before. I was only twenty-one when I had tried hard to build an idyllic home with Ira, a childhood friend. Films were not yet a frame for my experiences of love, but when a colleague leafed through my Raymond Carver to ask what I like to talk about when I talk about love, I promptly answered, 'There's this scene in *Apur*

Sansar, the best film I ever saw. Apu and Aparna are married. One morning, she wakes up to see that he has tied her saree to their bedcover. She smacks Apu on his back. Still groggy, he plays with her hairpin, and then reaches for his pack of cigarettes. She has left him a note inside—"Only one after meals. You've promised." His smile drips contentment. For me, that moment, that smile, is love.' My mornings with Ira were never quite so sublime. If I woke up after her, she would often be livid. She'd send me outside to smoke and I'd have to brush my teeth if I wanted to kiss her after. Aparna is frugal. She protests when Apu insists they travel in a carriage instead of a tram. Ira's parsimony, however, was more oppressive. In a month, I could only buy two books, and unlike Aparna, Ira never took my matches to gently light my cigarette.

To expect that reality will come to mimic art is a desire that is foolish, and also tyrannical. Ray had made me believe that the simple act of saying 'yes' would help me chance upon a present that would correct the deficiencies of my past. If I was Apu, I should have surely found an Aparna in Ira and Kamya. The ridiculousness of this assumption never really became apparent to me, not when I moved out of the flat I shared with Ira, nor when Kamya left our barsati with her mixer grinder. The domesticity Apu and Aparna share is perhaps only enchanted because it is short-lived. Aparna dies while giving birth to their son and Apu responds by rejecting the world. He stays in bed for days, grows a beard and finds solace in being peripatetic. He throws away his manuscript and sees its pages fly in a valley. Loneliness brings no redemption.

I was just as calamitous after breaking up with Kamya. I deleted all my emails, essays I had written for college, unedited articles and drafts of the novel I had hoped I would one day publish. Rather than remove the traces of Kamya that survived in my surroundings, rather than get rid of my curtains and her loofah, I tried removing all traces of myself from the world we inhabited. There is, in any separation, the inkling of death. Not only had I killed the hopes of a tomorrow Kamya and I had imagined—she was going to introduce me to her parents—I thought I'd also brutally killed my Aparna. In my manic stupor, I stood on our terrace in the middle of the night, howling and shrieking with regret. Days later, Kamya sent me lines written by the Pakistani poet Kyla Pasha: 'I've broken all these bottles on your doorstep, love / Walk softly— walk softly into the deep.' I had never felt more loved.

~

Blessed are the forgetful

When asked to explain bipolarity in terms that are relatable, I have always described it as an oscillation between mania and depression, a swing from plenitude to isolation. I have often been too embarrassed to confess that these opposites are not the only dualities I subscribe to. My thoughts are all fashioned by formulations whose structures are more childish and fundamental. I want only love, and am mortally petrified of hate. Still scared of bad consequences, I want to always remain good, but bipolarity has invariably forced me to trade in emotions I consider sinful and common—jealousy, anger, resentment. Jason, a college professor once pulled me aside to say, 'You need to realize that it's never a case of just this *or*

that. You can only arrive at freedom when you acknowledge
the capacities of this *and* that.' Every time I have had a quarrel
with a lover, when I've been forced to accept that life and
love are messy, that there might be three meanings to words
instead of two, I have tried hard to follow Jason's direction.
I must confess that I have mostly failed.

Mania and depression both necessitate a metamorphosis,
and my forged, immoderate selves often refuse to coexist. My
Dr Jekyll can only repent for the excesses of my Mr Hyde. A
friend once told me, 'The trouble with your mania is that we see
another Shreevatsa we never knew existed, and the trouble with
the depressed Shreevatsa is that he is nothing like the affable
Shreevatsa we loved.' I have since relied on docility when atoning
for the vulgar overconfidence of my manic spells and the dour
dullness of my depression. I find a certain assurance in being
deferential. The apple cart of affection and fondness is unwieldy,
and I rarely want to do anything to topple it. This agreeability is
fragile, though, and like love, it begs to be shattered.

I was in the throes of depression when Rachel sent me
three books she had read to better understand the patterns
of my bipolarity. Lovers had often googled my condition
and acquainted themselves with the effects of my affliction,
but only Rachel said she was also interested in its cause. I
hadn't even opened her books when I called her to say, 'Why
are you patronizing me like this? Bipolarity is something I
live with every day. I don't need to read about it too.' For
weeks, I had compensated for my depression by feigning an
investment. I was tired of my disguise. She had little idea
I had considered swallowing my flatmate's box of sleeping
pills or that I had begun to find our future impossible.

'You're being unfair,' she said. 'I was only trying to help.'

I snapped. 'I want someone who will love me, not a Florence Nightingale who cares.'

In *The Book of Laughter and Forgetting*, Milan Kundera has a word of caution for those who fall helplessly in love— 'Oh lovers! Be careful in those dangerous first days! Once you've brought breakfast in bed, you'll have to bring it forever, unless you want to be accused of lovelessness and betrayal.' Panicked by the prospect of that accusation, I have tried hard to make that initial flush of passion and discovery last the course of a relationship. Expectedly, my attempts have proved futile. Soured by the precariousness of my moods, my Eden, once lost, has proved impossible to find. In my experiences of love, there has only ever been good or evil.

I remember I was depressed when Lucia spoke of rainy nights in Himachal, hurried walks in Benares and endless cups of tea in Falmouth. I cut her short. 'Can't you see, Luce? I've fallen too far from the tree. You can't take me back to paradise.' Depression, I found, removed me from the very memories my mania would furiously varnish.

The time when Lucia came to see me in India, she stayed for twelve days. On her last night in the country, we decided to watch *Eternal Sunshine of the Spotless Mind*. Exhausted, her belly flustered by the kebab I'd fed her, she soon fell asleep. She sadly missed the best part. With her head on my shoulder, I finished watching a film I had already devoured over a dozen times.

You frown when you are depressed, but the slouch lasts longer. Waking up is not easy, and going to work is yet more difficult. Joel Barish doesn't want to get out of bed.

His shoulders tell that story. He leaves home with some purpose, but finds that the drive to the office is too long. He calls in sick, and gets on a train instead. I have known Joel's desolation ever since I was a teenager. Unduly sombre when I was a boy of sixteen, I would ignore three alarm clocks every morning. To distract myself from schoolwork, I had found on the shelves of our living room *The Complete Works of Swami Vivekananda*. As I tried reading each word of its nine volumes, my father lauded me for an effort he considered both noble and Herculean. My despair only grew. Wanting to be a monk, I vowed to stay celibate. My hormones, however, raged against my resolve. Desire would get the better of me on some nights, and so to castigate myself, I'd take unending walks. My 1999 journal reads like a tabloid of torment.

Joel too keeps a journal in which he writes as much as he sketches. One of the first entries he reads tells us why the winter we see is still so bleak. It is February, but more tragically for Joel, it is Valentine's Day. He writes, 'Today is a holiday invented by greeting card companies to make people feel like crap.' This gripe couldn't be any more familiar. Embittered and frustrated, my sixteen-year-old self would also view 14 February as a conspiracy. Chastity, I then found, doesn't just foment depression, it also imitates it. You do want to be left alone by the world, but you simultaneously, and somewhat desperately, want it to reach out too. You want someone to alleviate your alienation. All your continence really needs is a woman's hug. Standing on a beach, Joel can't make eye contact with Clementine, but when she waves in his direction, he scribbles, 'Why do I fall in love with every woman I see who shows me the least bit of attention?' My willpower was equally feeble.

An old-age home, unlike the beach, is an unlikely place for an affair to start. Signing up as a volunteer, wanting to do my share of social work, my thoughts were pitifully chaste. It was with some earnestness that I'd change sheets, hang balloons and help infirm octogenarians walk, but my efforts at St Joseph's Home felt impassive until Mallika came along. Talkative, never hesitant to assert herself, her investment seemed fuller than mine. Mallika's conviviality, like Clementine's orange sweatshirt, was conspicuous. Joel is painfully awkward when Clementine first tries to strike up a conversation with him on a train. I too had stiffened when Mallika repeated a joke for me in the kitchen of the old-age home. I had my temperance to protect. She was fifteen, but spoke with authority. Thankfully, Mallika was relentless. She didn't stop with the cracks until I giggled. *Mallika*

Clementine invites Joel to her place for a drink. With the improbable soundtrack of Mohammed Rafi and Lata Mangeshkar playing in the background, she sidles up to the stranger on her couch and whispers drunkenly, 'I'm gonna marry you.' Joel blushes and hastily says he has to leave. Clementine writes her number on his hand, and once home, he doesn't take long to call her. She asks playfully, 'What took you so long?' With his shoulders hunched expectantly, he says, 'I just walked in.' It is perhaps the spontaneity of her next question—'You miss me?'—that lifts Joel's spirits fully. With a smile that is effortless, he replies, 'Oddly enough, I do.' Clementine cackles and says, 'You said "I do"! I guess that means we are married.' There is no affectation in Joel's toothy grin. We can tell they're in love.

After Mallika gave me her number, we started speaking on the phone for hours every day. My adolescence soon began to lose its dead weight. It didn't take us long to imagine the pleasures of matrimony. We wanted to have children. I had thought up names too. I began to find sustenance in the warm hugs and sudden kisses we'd steal in the minutes between private tuitions or on afternoons that were uninspected. In *Eternal Sunshine*, Clementine takes Joel to the Charles River for their 'honeymoon on ice'. The river is frozen, and while she skates and slips, Joel stands on the periphery, afraid of imperceptible cracks. She comes and gives him her hand, and it is in that simple and forgettable gesture that I find my defence of togetherness. As they lie on the river, Joel invents constellations for Clementine. Mallika and I found on the Hooghly a felicity the Charles seemingly affords. Our allowances would be spent hiring boats. In her cheer, I finally got over myself. Compared to celibate depression, romance offered a liberation that was fearless.

Written by Charlie Kaufman, *Eternal Sunshine* expectedly has surprises that are a tad absurd and postmodern. Joel and Clementine, we are told, have laid down on the Charles River before. It's just that they don't remember that moment. They had been lovers in the past, but their relationship had soured to the point that they'd bicker in flea markets. When eating out, they'd have very little to say to each other. Fittingly, Joel called them the 'dining dead'. These experiences, too charged and too many, would have usually been impossible to forget, but Kaufman invents a company—Lacuna Inc.—that does something fantastic. It allows you to delete from your memory a person you once loved. Memories, Lacuna believes, all have an emotional core, which once eradicated can cause the impressions left by an estranged other to disappear. Clementine is the first to sign up for an erasure that seems as painless as a CAT scan. Joel, tired of her impulsiveness and his mourning, soon follows.

Eternal Sunshine hits rewind even as it moves forward. Removing us from the present flirtations of Joel and Clementine—impromptu picnics, counting stars—the film goes back in time and takes us to the night Joel tried forgetting his Clem. Given how overwrought it leaves him, the memory of his break-up is protrusive enough for Lacuna's doctors to target first. Like all anxious lovers, Joel is waiting up for Clementine when she returns home in the middle of the night. She is drunk and he is jealous. Victimhood requires him to be uncharacteristically churlish when he accuses her of promiscuity. The relationship can't take the weight of this straw. Clementine takes her toothbrush and storms out. She is leaving him, and his belated remorse cannot invalidate the malice of his barb. *a micable breakup w Mallika*

The terms on which Mallika and I separated were relatively more amicable. Speaking to her from Cornwall, our sentences building up to a crescendo, my nineteen-year-old self felt glad we'd both have an opportunity to start afresh. The spectacle of a break-up, unfortunately, had only been postponed, not averted. Years later, we met in a Calcutta restaurant that was an experiment in Bollywood pastiche. My behaviour was similarly garish and distasteful. Freshly under the spell of mania, feeling as boorish as Joel once did, I told Mallika she had let me down. In language that was regrettably unsavoury, I accused her of fickleness and betrayal. The trouble

mania → bad ending

with mania's onset is that your ravings often still subscribe to reason. As you then indict and complain, your relations are undone by your invented logic. Sitting opposite Mallika, I launched into one pernicious diatribe after another. 'You don't know what love is,' I shouted out loud. The restaurant manager had turned his head.

Joel follows Clementine after she has walked through the door. He buys her a necklace, wanting forgiveness. He feels ashamed when ignored. Similarly, I felt reprehensible in the years Mallika and I didn't speak. The only apology I could muster—'That is not what I meant at all. That is not it, at all'—could not convey my regret. In mania, aggression precedes misgivings. A manic subject's anger, like that of an abandoned lover's, needs to be justified and the unconscious invariably finds it easy to distort histories of love and affection. Emotions are always simple prey. Unlike alcohol, imbalanced chemicals in the brain are no truth serums. The accusations I hurl are improvised only to authenticate a moral superiority my mania forces me to feel. I have unfairly admonished at least a dozen lovers and friends. My greatest sin, I believe, is the tawdriness of my fiction.

In cheerier times, Mallika and I used the poems of Pablo Neruda and Ogden Nash to communicate a love that, for the most part, remained light. She took me to the Calcutta Book Fair and together we bought the books of Lawrence Durrell, Sylvia Plath and Ted Hughes. Wanting to see our libraries settle on the same shelves one day, we inscribed these with both our names. Mallika had framed a picture of ours which I had kept on my desk long after I'd lost her affection. In my stupor, I removed each of these remnants. The doctors at Lacuna seem to know well the debilitation that objects accelerate. They ask Joel to get rid of anything that might remind him of Clementine. He takes to their office two bin liners that are stuffed with every memento he has—a snow globe, a Halloween skeleton, pages of his journal. I am better off. I still have the Neruda poems Mallika had earmarked.

I remain loyal to my memories of love. I protect them fiercely, scared that some numbing pill might soon have to be swallowed, or that depression lurks around the corner, waiting to wipe out or disfigure these souvenirs beyond recognition. I am mortified by the thought that I'll one day forget the tenderness with which Mallika called me Bunshi, a name my father had given me as a toddler. Joel feels a similar fear when the doctors of Lacuna—dressed in sinister white coats—take his mind back to moments when Clementine called him Joely, and he named her Tangerine. The memories he comes to inhabit he does not want erased. He wants to be with Clementine under a blanket again and hear her say, 'Joely, don't ever leave me.' Talking about how 'lonely it is to be a kid', she cries when describing her childhood insecurities. When she tells him she thought she was ugly, he kisses her repeatedly, and each time, he tells her she is pretty. Perhaps only love compensates for our lack.

Quite obviously a romantic comedy, *Eternal Sunshine*, is also a chase film. Joel tries hard to hide his memory of Clementine in corners of the unconscious where he thinks Lacuna's exterminators will not come looking. He makes her lie next to him in bed while his teenage self masturbates, only to be humiliated when his mother walks in. She goes with him to a time when he was four, crying for his mommy's attention. Desire, he casually admits, is strongest when it is

Oedipal. She holds his hand and takes him away when he is bullied by other children. Joel tells Clementine, 'I wish I knew you when I was a kid,' but he and I both know her protection is retrospective. Mallika's instincts were naturally maternal, and soon after she started calling me her boyfriend, she said she'd punch Satyah if she ever saw him. I felt consoled after I'd given her unfettered access to my haunted unconscious.

When Joel sits beside Clementine, eating takeaway noodles, he says, 'I can't remember anything without you.' Though I do find it a bit hard to forgive the mush, my own sweet nothings, I confess, have been equally mawkish. I have found redemption in the thoughtless exchanges of love, and like Joel, I have found elation and struggle in surrender. I watched *Eternal Sunshine* two years after Mallika and I separated, but I found in the film an assurance that the joys of an adolescent love were possible even in adulthood. To free Joel of Clementine, Lacuna has to expunge the memory of the day they first met. Shy and distant, Joel is eating alone at a picnic. Clementine sits next to him, asks him if she can take a piece of his chicken, and then picks it up without waiting for an answer. The familiarity of that one gesture makes Joel feel they 'were already lovers'. His reticence, though, has more to do with monogamy than personality. He happens to be living with a woman named Naomi.

In 2006, I sat in my office chair, tired by the demands of my live-in relationship, when my colleague Madhavi came up from behind and used Holi as an excuse to smear my cheeks pink. 'Your shirts are all blue. You looked like you could do with some colour in your life.'

I laughed and said, 'I didn't know my wardrobe was being noticed.'

Her smile was flirtatious. 'I was too bored not to.'

We soon started following each other out for cigarettes by the fire exit. I repeated to her lines from one of my favourite poems, 'One Cigarette' by Edwin Morgan: 'You are here again, and I am drunk on your tobacco lips.'

Taking a drag of her Navy Cut, she said, 'To a smoker, that's too obvious a pickup line.' Madhavi spared my ego when cutting me down to size. 'I just want to see you up that game,' she smiled.

'It's been a while since I've been in the game,' I confessed.

'Tobacco lips, though. You haven't forgotten how to play.' In just three days, I had moved out of the flat I shared with Ira.

Our romance followed a standard that was very *Eternal*. We never entered or left the office at the same time, and we invented fictitious lovers to satisfy the curiosity of colleagues who'd always become inquisitive at the sight of love bites. The passenger seat of Madhavi's green Santro became home. When she took out her guitar to play a Pink Floyd tune or to sing a Bob Dylan song, I would always demand an encore. With her, I felt free of family, its trauma and its expectation. Waiting for her in a cafe, I'd spend my time reading, underlining passages she might find amusing or poignant. I was finishing Milan Kundera's *Slowness* when she walked in. I had found my quote of the day—'Love is by definition an unmerited gift; being loved without meriting it is the very proof of real love.' Madhavi took my copy, read it in a night, and by the next day, she had written a review for our paper.

Linguistic dexterity often gives manic subjects away. Their sentences defy punctuation. It is hard to put a comma to their thoughts, and they certainly do not respect the full stop. With a ready and inexhaustible stock of repartees, they can tire you with their ceaseless conversations. For me, comebacks were a lot more fun when I sat opposite Madhavi in restaurants, willingly sharing the vegetarian food she ordered. We never were the 'dining dead'. Over Thai green curry, I once told her, 'Every woman is a book whose pages I want to tear and eat.' Unruffled by the depravity of my desire, she told me if she could turn herself into a book, she would wait for me at a coffee table.

Our break-up in 2007 might have been a touch acrimonious, but every time I have started riding the crest of a manic high since that year, I've called Madhavi, and have invariably started my conversations with an 'I love you'. I know these confessions are interruptive, but the extent of her affection has left me entitled. Once, just before we hung up, she laughed and said, 'You're a crazy little bastard.'

Joel can't stop the crafty doctors from erasing Clementine, but fate and an unconscious belonging again take him to her couch, and they again listen to Lata's 'Wada Na Tod'. Lacuna, though, despite its thoroughness, messes up. Joel and Clementine soon discover they are former lovers, not new sweethearts, that they have felt a similar flush in the past, and that things had not ended well the last time. They stand in Joel's hallway and ask where they can go from here. Their history has made Clementine wary, but Joel asks her to wait. He shrugs dismissively when she says she'll get bored of him, and suddenly, they laugh. While Kaufman reminds us of Nietzsche—'Blessed are the forgetful, for they get the better even of their blunders'—I think of Kundera instead. All I've ever wanted from love is laughter, forgetting and a second chance. The bitterness of our parting behind us, the pain of institutionalization behind me, Madhavi once reached for a postcard I used as a bookmark and wrote on its back, 'Repeat after me. I'll not go to the loony bin again.' We laughed like only old lovers can.

So what do we do?

Having observed me over a weekend, surprised by how uncontrollably my fingers trembled, disappointed after a string of my responses had been trite and dim-witted, a friend described me as 'sluggish'. That single word, which to me was a damning indictment, ensured that my 2011 did not begin well. I began to chide myself for waking up at noon every day. I hated myself for not being funny. The weight my medicines caused me to gain had even forced me to buy a new pair of jeans. In June, when I decided to tailor my psychiatrist's prescription and taper my lithium, the only precedent I could cite was again cinematic.

Of the many reasons why *Garden State* stayed with me since I first watched it in 2005, one was admittedly patriotic. The quirky romantic comedy starts with a dream of its protagonist and we see Andrew Largeman sitting in the middle seat of a flight that is close to crashing. As passengers scream and oxygen masks drop from their hatches, we hear a Sanskrit chant being sung in praise of Ganesha. I could tell this was the start of something good.

A message waits for the twenty-five-year-old Andrew on his answering machine when he wakes up. His mother has just died. After nine years of staying away, he will now have to go home. Andrew opens a mirror cabinet and we see its shelves all lined with medicine bottles, but the first pill we see him swallow is one of ecstasy. Playing spin-the-bottle at a house party can considerably mitigate the grief of that morning's funeral. Still hung over, Andrew meets Sam in the waiting room of a doctor's office the next day. He had played the role of a retarded quarterback in a forgettable film, but she recognizes him instantly. There is warmth in her incessant chatter, and when she gives him her headphones to listen to a song—'New Slang' by The Shins—we discover a rare compassion in music.

There is something common about the wish that doctors will diagnose us by saying, 'There's absolutely nothing wrong with you.' Dr Cohen oddly delivers this verdict well before he has looked at Andrew's charts. When he does start scanning his patient's medical history, however, he seems perturbed. Raising his eyebrows, he asks incredulously, 'Lithium? Depakote? Have these helped you at all?'

I had of course come to know these medicines well, and like Andrew, I yearned to say, 'No. As a matter of fact, it recently occurred to me that there might not be anything wrong with me.'

Dr Cohen, a doctor I immediately idolized, says he can prescribe pills that'll help any residue of past medicine leave Andrew's body. 'Seeing all the lithium you're on, it's amazing you can even hear me right now.' Andrew isn't bipolar, but I didn't stop to acknowledge that fact. When he said he was taking a 'vacation' from his regime of medication, I felt my own indiscretions had Dr Cohen's assent.

Christmas is never a good time for someone who was once convinced he was the Second Coming. Invited to Rohini's house for a party on Christmas Eve, having skipped my dose of lithium again, I decided to test the limits of my new-found abandon. She opened the door to hear me announce, 'I have converted to Islam.'

I was quoting the three verses of the Koran I had memorized, when she stopped me and said, 'I believe you. I'd never put whimsy past you.' I lost the resolve to continue my ridiculous charade after we started playing truth-or-dare. I really did need some alcohol then.

A month later, the chair I was given in my Bombay office was right next to hers. Paul Auster helped break the ice which hadn't melted. I gave her three of his books, and she brought me a David Sedaris—*Me Talk Pretty One Day*. 'Watch me. One day,' she said, leaving the book on my desk. When she made me listen to The Black Keys, Macklemore and Alt-J on my headphones, I felt a dash of relief. Rohini was more Sam, less Aparna.

Like Sam and Andrew, much of the affinity that Rohini and I came to share was strengthened in the presence of my best friend. Our intimacy almost always had an audience. Deliberately finding an excuse to accompany each other on our journalistic assignments, we met mentalists, chefs and one particularly industrious American brewer. The narrative of our togetherness was populated by at least two dozen cameos whose backstory gave our little romantic comedy a distinct prologue. Taking Rohini to meet Abhinav, a brilliant former colleague, I had never imagined his walk-on part would eventually prove to be catalytic. After he had entertained us for over two hours with his novel interpretations of Joseph Campbell's *The Hero with a Thousand Faces* and Dostoevsky's *Crime and Punishment*, I asked in a whisper, 'Abhinav, do you have some cannabis you could maybe spare?' The skill with which I separated marijuana seeds from stems later that evening led Rohini to say, 'It doesn't look like you've been out of practice.' It had been three years since I had rolled a joint. Strangely, my capitulation only needed that one full drag.

The crotchety lady who lived on a pavement outside our office always had cannabis hidden in the folds of her saree. I thought the supply was providential, and soon enough, the daily prescription of weed I was writing myself stopped coming with a cap. Rohini had made me lose that crippling awareness of the kilos I had piled on, and marijuana, I was convinced, was causing me to quickly lose all that weight. With no mood stabilizers in my body, I began to stay up nights, and Rohini and I soon began savouring each other's insomnia.

In *Garden State*, Andrew's father is his psychiatrist, and the plot of the film makes fairly clear that any such doubling up should be prohibited. As Rohini critiqued my writing and I hers, we tried to prove wrong the assumption that lovers cannot be each other's editors. We would travel the city for eggs at the crack of dawn. We'd buy her new T-shirts so she could skirt a walk of shame in the office, and we'd find a comparable joy in gossip and Angela Carter.

Sitting on a bar stool, Andrew once tells Sam, 'The only thing I ever liked doing is pretending to be someone else, but the only parts I get are those of handicapped people.' I didn't even have to tweak this quote for it to be applicable. Sam talks about her own epilepsy to prove the benefits of laughter and forgetting. She collects his tears in a paper cup. Without ever belittling my condition, Rohini forced me not to be apologetic about a fate I couldn't revise. Her humour made it impossible for me to infect our love with my melancholy. One night, our mood buoyed by rum, whisky, cannabis and a rerun of *Modern Family*, Rohini and I suddenly started talking about the allure of winter weddings in Delhi. We had only been together a few weeks, but we found we had little trouble discussing a possible guest list and the availability of caterers. I asked her if she'd like to marry me. The next morning, I called friends and my father to say she had said yes. They were circumspect. 'You've been here before,' they told me.

'This is madness,' said Rohini, 'so let's just keep it secret.' Andrew and Sam had chalked their love story in just four days. Rohini and I had taken four months.

In its last sequence, *Garden State* exchanges its charming eccentricity for drama that is decidedly Hollywood. The setting of an airport again becomes a metaphor for transition. In a hurry to catch his flight, Andrew tells Sam he has much to figure out, that she should look at his departure as an ellipsis, not an end. Rohini had grown used to the ellipsis. We'd broken up twice because I'd claimed I still had to know myself. I struggled with the idea of permanence, and the fluctuations of my non-medicated and drugged mind would intermittently make it hard for me to keep my promise.

After Andrew has impulsively disembarked, he kisses Sam and tells her, 'I don't want to waste any more of my life without you in it.' Chastened by solitude, I'd come back to repeat a variation of this sentiment to Rohini, and each time, she'd take me back.

But then, in May 2013, I went and crossed a line. Unable to cope with the pressures of work, and with marijuana exaggerating the volatility of chemicals in my brain, I had again become familiar with the aggression of mania. I called Rohini to accuse her of desertion, infidelity and hypocrisy. I had no proof to substantiate any of these claims. This separation was more final. There would be no forgiveness. She said in a mail, 'Right now I don't even know if you're okay or not. I am so goddamn fucking tired of being abandoned by you.'

Garden State ends with a question. Having upturned his life for Sam, Andrew asks her, 'So what do we do?' Though this line forces you to acknowledge the economy of his achievement and the uncertainties of their future, it has always inspired in me a nostalgia. Comprehending little of the Vedanta philosophy I read when I was sixteen, I did remain fascinated by a two-word question that kept appearing in the writings of Adi Shankaracharya—'*Tataḥ kiṁ?* What then?' In a diary I kept at the time I was dating Rohini, I wrote on 25 May 2013, 'If my imagination had not exhausted our future, would I still be asking, "Tataḥ kiṁ, tataḥ kiṁ?" Tell me, where would we have gone from here?'

Though I left Rohini with words that were pathetic—'It's hard to be happy when there is nothing to be sure of'—I had already given up on grace a week before. My conversations with other women had turned nimble. I was undoubtedly projecting my guilt of infidelity when I told Rohini that she had betrayed me with men I imagined she had met at a recent party. Years later, however, I would try assuaging my troubled conscience with a delusion. By divorcing myself, I had protected her from the carnage of my mania that was about to worsen. She hadn't been forced to comprehend my paranoia of being followed by the country's intelligence establishment. I hadn't called her for counsel when I quit my job at a Delhi newspaper, pretending to be a renegade. As I was carried away, raging and shrieking, by doctors of the Fortune Foundation, she hadn't had to suffer with me the violence of that moment or the anxieties of an incarceration that would last three months.

5

I Am Shiva

My family only ever holidayed in places of pilgrimage. For us, the 2001 Kumbh Mela was the vacation of a lifetime. On our way to Allahabad, we stopped in Benares, and the city, I thought, had only its architecture to offer at three in the morning. An hour earlier, when my uncle had woken me up, saying, 'I'm going to show you the real Benares,' I had sensed an adventure. He had let me taste bhang for the first time earlier that evening, and at sixteen, I felt I was again being given access to pleasures that were illicit. This time, I was having fun. The narrow lane that leads up to the Kashi Vishwanath Temple can seem endless when its teeming shops have their shutters down, and especially when sleep laminates your eyes. When I asked how long I would have to walk, my *mausa* just said, 'It'll be worth it.'

A few feet away from the temple, I was asked to deposit in a locker my belt, watch and wallet. I looked quizzically at my father who had also accompanied us. 'In the court of Pashupatinath, the Lord of the Herds,' he explained, 'animals are brought to life, so you don't take dead ones inside.' I held my jeans in place with my fingers, and stepping inside Kashi Vishwanath, I found its lack of ostentation peculiar. I was being made to pray to Vishnu and Ganesha—'Please make Mallika love me forever'—when I heard the sound of cymbals and bells fill the compound. My father led me to the temple's sanctum. He held my hand. I let him. I'd stopped caring for my adult pretences.

Hymns that are sung in praise of Shiva can often be more percussive than mellifluous. A pause is an opportunity for a start that is yet more emphatic. Hearing chants that rose as quickly as they dipped, I suddenly felt wide awake. Standing at the door, I could see half a dozen priests, their bare bodies impervious to the January cold. Initially, the chamber was dark, but as the six ash-smeared men dropped camphor in the lamps they held, the room lit up. I soon began to feel an insidious fear. Shiva was angry in the stories I had heard, and in the fervour of the priests and the bang of their cymbals, I sensed fury, not rapture. I'd always believed that Shiva, the God of Destruction, demands pacification, but in that moment, I had no piety to offer. As the chants built up to their climax, I felt death was palpable, and then inexplicably, I began to feel aroused.

As we stood outside, buckling our belts, my mausa told me that the *mangala aarti* is auspicious because it is liminal. 'Day and night are almost simultaneous at this hour,' he said. 'If Shiva didn't drink the darkness, there would be no light.' The explanation, though poetic, felt invented. I was still mystified by the concurrence of horror and pleasure. Fear was rendered erotic that morning, and when my father interrupted my reverie to ask what I was thinking, I didn't have the audacity to say, 'Death and sex.' For the first time in sixteen years, I had chanced upon a notion, which despite its transience, seemed authentic, even novel. In the several trips I've made to Benares since, I have chased that slippery sentience. Standing outside the Vishwanath sanctum again, sitting on the edge of crematoriums, watching the Ganga in the light of a full moon, I've felt more greedy than nostalgic.

In 2015, I met a Sanskrit scholar in Benares who spoke about death with an irreverence I sorely wanted to ape. Amitabha Bhattacharya was sitting in his cubicle of an office when he said, 'In the rest of the world's cities, everyone is trying to survive, but they're ultimately dying. In Benares, everyone is waiting for death. People have nothing to be afraid of here.'

With all the sincerity I could muster, I asked, 'So there is pleasure to be found in death?'

He got up to spit the juices of his paan on the pavement outside. 'For that,' he smiled, 'you'll have to be either a devotee or a hedonist.' He looked dissatisfied, though, and soon went on to add, 'But if there was pleasure in dying, there'd be no joy in living. We'd all be suicidal.' Lighting our cigarettes an hour later, he said with a laugh. 'You're right. There's certainly some pleasure in dying, after all.'

Leaving Bhattacharya's office that evening, I instinctively thought of Albert Camus. In *A Happy Death*, he writes, 'Sometimes it takes more courage to live than to shoot yourself.' Much of my late adolescence and early adulthood had been spent devising a death that would be novelistic. Benares had finally given me cause to wait, but as I kept walking through its many lanes, I felt I had brought the wrong compass with me. I was using Camus and Nietzsche—'The

living being is only a species of the dead'—to understand a
city that was ostensibly Shiva's. Compared to the colour of
crematoriums, Western thought had begun to seem a touch
too black-and-white. Despite my many visits to the city, I
had failed to grasp Kashi's significance. I was a tourist. A
month later, however, I found on the shelves of a Calcutta
bookshop an early edition of Diana L. Eck's *Banaras: City
of Light*. Reading the author's introduction, I sat transfixed.
When I chanced upon the line 'Death in Kashi is death
known and faced, transformed and transcended,' I felt I had
found my missing grail.

Defying the directive of my psychiatrist, I didn't sleep
that night. Pinned to my reading chair, I barely looked up.
Banaras was astonishing in its precision and staggering in its
scope. Pouring us cups of chai, a politician in Benares had once
quoted Mark Twain with some glee—'Benares is older than
history, older than tradition, older even than legend.' Diana
Eck, though, gave me a more delicious bite of the American
writer to chew. 'The town is a vast museum of idols—and
all of them crude, misshapen, and ugly. They flock through
one's dreams at night, a wild mob of nightmares,' Twain
had written. This disbelieving gaze of Westerners gave my
own incredulity a precedent, but Eck, unlike Twain, seemed
more interested in seeing Kashi through the eyes of a believer,
through a lens more Hindu.

Having just married Parvati, Shiva, like a typical besotted
groom, wanted to find for his wife a new home, a place less
torturous than the Himalayas. So he left Kailasa for Kashi.
Benares effectively became the city where the most reclusive
of all ascetics was domesticated. In the temple compound, a

priest had once pointed to the site of the Jnana Vapi, and said, 'If we hadn't hidden Shiva here, we would never have been able to keep him safe from the Mughals.' I admittedly found myself more captivated by the story Eck had to tell. Using his trident, Shiva dug the earth to create Jnana Vapi himself. He had to find a way to cool his own linga. Eck's observation— 'Mythology becomes geography'—seemed pithy only because she was such a diligent cartographer. Halfway through the book, I arrived at the chapter 'The Sun and the Adityas'. Eck starts by quoting a hymn from the Rig Veda. It reads: 'Arise! The breath of life hath come back to us, / The darkness is gone, the light approacheth!' I looked out of my window to see a pink sky. The sun was about to rise. This synchronicity was striking not just because of its symmetry, but because it was liminal too.

~

In January 2016, my editor shouted from her end of the office, 'Diana Eck is coming to Bombay. You're interviewing her next week.' My euphoria, which had begun to border on mania that month, was now impossible to contain. 'This alone makes journalism worth it,' I said, while thanking her profusely. In the days to follow, the *Banaras* author would again make me an insomniac. When asked why I was staying up nights, preparing for an interview that would only last twenty minutes, I told a colleague, somewhat hysterically, 'The thing about Eck is she facilitates awakenings.' The neurotic order of my room had been upset by half a dozen books I'd begun to highlight furiously. Next to Eck's *Banaras*,

India: A Sacred Geography and *Encountering God*, I'd leave open Devdutt Pattanaik's *7 Secrets of Shiva*, Roberto Calasso's *Ka* and Wendy Doniger's *The Hindus: An Alternative History*. I felt Shiva was revealing himself to me in language. Bombay *was* Benares.

On the morning of 18 January, I reached the Bombay Yacht Club. As I waited for one of my favourite authors in the lobby, I was frightened by the possibility that I might not be able to mask my devotion. Mania often forces my agnosticism to quickly dissipate, and in its place I discover a reservoir of faith which fast threatens to turn delusive. Thankfully, my fervour had not quite overtaken reason when I got up to shake hands with my hero, Harvard professor of comparative religion and Indian studies, Diana L. Eck. She admitted she was tired and I confessed I hadn't slept. After I told her about how the sun had once synched itself with her book, she busied herself with the etymology of my name. I apologized for being a fan.

The professor distilled the purpose of the humanities—'It is to try and understand and articulate what the world looks like to someone else'—and then drew a subtle distinction between plurality and pluralism. Plurality, she said, is just a fact, while 'pluralism is something you have to create and participate in'. She spoke about Donald Trump with a prescience that would soon define liberal thought—'He is against everything America stands for and is.' In *India: A Sacred Geography*, Eck had written, 'Globalisation has been good for the gods.' When I asked her how, she started talking about the ease with which someone in a Harvard dorm room can sponsor a puja at Sri Venkateswara Temple in Tirumala. I cut her short. 'But then you can also be in the same dorm room and join ISIS?' She looked surprised, and I'd startled myself.

As she described the lanes and ghats of Kashi, I hung on to her every word, and then, suddenly, when talking about how Shiva had pervaded the very presence of Benares, she said in an accent that was entirely unaffected, 'Kashi ke kankar, Shiv Shankar.' She explained, 'This demonstrates the idea that the very clay of Kashi is Shiva.' The utterance of 'Shiva' and 'Kashi' had become an invocation for me, and I soon came to revere Eck as a priestess, a custodian. The next day when I went to hear her deliver a lecture on India's sacred rivers, I removed my belt, watch and wallet. I was again barefoot in the court of Pashupatinath. My devotion had created this temple. I was far gone.

For almost every place she mentioned that evening, Eck had brought with her a slide. Watching her photographs of Haridwar, Vrindavan and Gangotri, I thought of the Kumbh Mela in Allahabad. At an hour that believers considered propitious, my father and I had taken a boat to the Triveni Sangam, a point of confluence where Shiva's Ganga and Krishna's Yamuna met the now mythical Saraswati. I naturally conjured the crucifix when I was told, 'Taking a single dip will wash you of all your sins.' When Eck called the Ganga 'a theatre', I stood on my toes, and hoped my own quiet drama would draw her attention for a moment. The Ganga, in her description, was embracing, nourishing and vital, but the river I had known was first a lover.

In *Ka*, Roberto Calasso writes, 'Of no other woman was Parvati so jealous as of Ganga.' As her sister's waters dripped down Shiva's face, Parvati is said to have angrily asked her husband, 'Who is that damn woman hiding in your hair?' Her indignation was justified, for 'even his saliva smacked of Ganga'. I had always been fascinated by Shiva's celestial conjugality, but the ruses of his divine and secret love affair left me enchanted. My grandmother had told me the story of Ganga's origin with a fervid piety. Ganga, an irresistible force, had to first collide with Shiva, an immovable object, for the earth to withstand her velocity. I had often thought of Shiva adjusting the crescent moon in his locks, his body stiffening, as he anticipated an impact that would first be fierce, but eventually comforting. As I heard Eck speak, I remembered that for all of 2012, I had refused to stand under a shower. I was no Shiva, and was afraid of the violence water might inflict. Besides, I had no dreadlocks. I was balding.

Forty minutes into the lecture, I saw an ageing man walking like my grandfather, with a hunch and a walking stick. He was finding it hard to navigate the packed hall. Though the question I then asked myself—'What would Shiva do?'—was undoubtedly comical, it helped me act with a purpose that was unfeigned. I wore my slippers and walked up to him. 'I can't find my wife,' he said nervously.

I suggested we sit on the chairs outside and wait. 'She'll find us once this is done,' I assured him and held his hand. The octogenarian told me he was a doctor, and when I admitted it had recently become hard for me to sleep, he instantly grew animated.

'I'm also a yoga instructor, and what you need to do is hold your right hand like this,' he instructed, while holding his index and middle finger down with his thumb. As he led me through the various poses of Pranayama, I could hear Eck sing a hymn in Sanskrit. My masters had begun to arrive all at once, and when the doctor introduced me to his wife by saying, 'This boy is a godsend,' I wanted to smile. His wife said she recognized me. She'd read my name in the paper. They invited me for tea, and I soon discovered a new majesty.

As an adolescent, I'd giggled when a priest told me the story of Shiva's linga, but as a student of literature, I later found in it a thrill that was delectably Dionysiac. Infuriated by sages who thought he was coveting their wives, Shiva sought to end the quarrel by castrating himself, and that is how his phallus fell, flaming, discarded and wonderful. In this sacrifice, believers find benevolence, but the moral, I have found, obfuscates the story. For a god who is called Ardhanarishvara because he is perfectly androgynous, who can burn desire when he sees it lurking in the bushes, such an act of self-mutilation was surely one of indifference first. The joy of detachment is that it makes everything dispensable. Predictably, for Shiva, the Lord of Excess, even aloofness becomes an extreme position.

I had always wanted Shiva's stoicism, but that night, walking the streets of Bombay, I was far from impassive. I oddly wanted to feel his terror. In my interview with Diana Eck, she had told me, 'Most of the great Shaiva temples began because a devotee created a Shiva linga, and had such great devotion that Shiva appeared to him or her. It's devotion that creates a place. The symbolic is too complicated to take literally.' Coming across a Shiva temple in India isn't exactly fortuitous—there's one on the corner of most roads—but when I saw a Shiva linga hidden in a tiled white enclosure, under the aegis of a peepul tree, I thought providence was only effective when divine. It had been a while since I had prayed, and even though I had begun to imitate the faithful, I remained obstinate. God, I had for long believed, was entertained by dialogue, not discourse.

'I am not here to ask for anything,' I said in a whisper as I folded my hands, 'I'm only here to understand.' My grandmother had taught me how to stand in a temple, and my manic mind was only waiting to be flooded by all the stories she had taken relish in retelling.

Brahma and Vishnu, my dadi had once told me, were prone to squabbling. With no neutral judge to arbitrate, they each tried desperately to convince the other of their supremacy. One day, when this dispute grew particularly petty, a shaft of light pierced the three worlds of the universe. 'It had no beginning and no end,' she said, 'and from this light emerged Shiva, the Supreme One.'

Standing in front of a piece of stone that had been consecrated under a peepul tree, I said to Shiva's linga, 'I'm inside your light, not outside it. When you open your third eye, you see no distinction. I don't either. I am you. You are me.' My devotion had given way to Icarus's bluster. I wanted to play chess with my deity and get pummelled by him in a boxing ring. Five weeks on, as I was being injected with a sedative by a sloppy medic, I regretted not having feared his worst.

~

Symptoms of mania are often common enough for those on the outside to conclude that bipolarity affects all its sufferers equally. Watching the film *Michael Clayton*, I too found it hard to escape the notion that all we manic-depressives witnessed a similar beauty and fought the same beasts. In his manic euphoria, Arthur Edens, a leading attorney, thinks it wise to strip in a deposition room. Tom Wilkinson plays Arthur with a deftness I thought was uncanny. Confined in a police station, he is visited by Michael, whose industry George Clooney captures with rolled sleeves and a stern gaze.

Arthur is rambling hysterically, but even though the pace of his speech might be hard to chase, his logic isn't. 'The time is now, this moment today,' he tells Michael. 'There's a reason you're here.' Not only does Arthur fetishize his audience, he also idealizes his litigant—'She is God's perfect little creature.' After railing against crimes committed by an agricultural conglomerate, he then raves about Lithuanian prostitutes. He has gone off his medication, so his veracity is hard to trust. When Michael pulls out a bottle of pills, Arthur flinches. 'Everything is finally significant. The world is a beautiful and radiant place,' he says. Things escalate, and Michael shouts, 'You're a manic-depressive.' With a conviction I've known too well, Arthur straightens up to reply, 'I am Shiva, the God of Death.'

If bipolarity had to be assigned a god, Shiva would certainly be the obvious choice. Meditating for centuries on end, he finds an oblivion every depressive craves. Sitting in their chairs and lying on their couches, disconsolate patients have tired therapists with the refrain, 'Only if this world would stop existing.' This propensity, for me, metamorphoses into conceit when rage tints my mania: 'I can stop this world from existing.'

While secretly swaying to my soundtrack for an apocalypse, I have again thought I was Shiva, dancing his *tandav* of destruction. The precariousness of my mental health perpetuates many Shaivite myths. During my manic breakdowns, my mood sometimes swings with a rapidity that makes wonder and anger, good and bad, bliss and sorrow, seem simultaneous. Seated on a cushion in a friend's house, I was captivated by an image of Shiva he worshipped every day. For the first time, I was in awe of both the moon in Shiva's hair and the hissing snake around his neck. Here was dread that came laced with beauty. I surreptitiously hid the picture in my bag. I had stolen fire and the god.

When gods and demons churned the oceans for the nectar of immortality, the water spewed a poison so deadly that the world feared annihilation. Elixirs, legends suggest, almost always have to be counterbalanced. Shiva, for whom eradication is sometimes a prerogative, came by to drink the venom with a nonchalance that diners reserve for their sodas. That poison is said to still swim in the god's neck, making it blue, giving him the name Nilakantha, the One with the Blue Neck. Clenching my throat, hoping my neck too would turn a dark indigo, my suffering has been hard to swallow and my anger impossible to spit out. The pain of abuse can intensify if looked at as a microcosm of the world's ills, but once made a common metaphor, it is diminished. Shiva's immunity, I believed, was transferable. Manic for the first time, I told a friend I would be unaffected by future adversity, and when my mother said, 'If you smoke so much, you could get lung cancer, or worse, throat cancer,' my laugh was cocky. 'But that would not be the end of the world,' I quipped.

Since that day, my mother has been cold to the blackness of my humour. When her father passed away, I paid my last respects by kneeling before his body, lifting my hands in the air and chanting 'Allah hu Akbar' to myself. My response wasn't secular, it was maniacal. Rituals, Shiva had taught me, were meant to be disrupted. When leaving for the crematorium, my mother had instructed, 'Make sure the farewell you bid my father is fond.' She wasn't allowed to come keep an eye on me.

Unlike charitable incinerators, pyres cannot mask their violence. With the Ganga flowing behind me, I was hypnotized by the macabre reduction of a human body. Watching flesh become smoke and bone turn into soot, I did not once think of transience or the loss of my grandfather's affection. I could only think of Shiva's entourage, a retinue of ghosts, goblins and phantoms, for whom death was an occasion to revel and frolic. I wanted to smear myself with ash, get drunk on blood and dance like a delirious dervish. I grinned inanely that evening, wanting to balance the gloominess of faces I found unduly sombre. The wood used to fuel a pyre changes shape as quickly as the body it burns. My gaze was fixed on the skeleton of my grandfather's corpse when I noticed that the logs which held it together had come to resemble the frame of a bull. I thought I could see horns, a muzzle, the back and even a tail. I called my mother and said, 'Shiva has sent Nandi, his mount, his bull, his sentinel, to take Nanu.' She cried for her father. But more for her son.

A day later, when my grandfather's possessions were being distributed, I asked if I could have his two boxes of playing cards and poker chips. Parvati is said to have used dice to distract her husband from his predilections for reclusion and ruin, so when I began sorting my nana's spades and clubs, I thought it wise to leave the door of his room ajar. Tickled by my impudence, a distant cousin sat beside me to help. Mourners, I told her, are best diverted by an exhibition of whimsy and chance. 'You're crazy,' she said, 'but fun crazy. I like that.'

~

Scriptures suggest that the avatars of a single god are dissimilar because the world's demands shift with every epoch. Rama's virtuosity, for instance, makes him venerable, but in times substantially greyer, it is Krishna's craftiness that comes to seem more relatable. When manic subjects delude themselves into believing that they too are incarnations of Jesus, Vishnu or Shiva, however, their flights of fancy are fantastic, but their actions also betray a failure of imagination. They convince themselves their interventions are divine, but miracles, they forget, are dramatic only when performed once. The repetition of a predecessor's heroics is more proof of mimicry. After a messy break-up, I called the father of an ex to accuse him of dereliction and corruption. My anger, sadly, was unoriginal. Shiva, I remembered as I picked up the phone, was never quite the model son-in-law.

The cliché is patriarchal, but Shiva, like the average Indian husband, was not effusive when Sati, his first wife, announced she would leave his Himalayan sanctuary to visit her father. Daksha, from the look of things, was performing a grand sacrifice, but had failed to include Shiva in his guest list. They had never really got along, Daksha and Shiva, and the usually profuse Shiva was reticent when his wife made her little declaration. The all-seeing god could smell death from a mountain away. He sounded resigned when he said, 'Go if you must.' The reception she was given was not warm. Insults began to flow thick and fast. The crowd grew hostile, and Daksha had a thing or two to add. Sati's husband, the Lord of the Abject, was easy to castigate. Her patience running thin, Sati immolated herself, and hers became the grand sacrifice.

Inconsolable and enraged, Shiva turned the home of his in-laws into a site of massacre. Blood was spilt, stones were thrown, bodies were dragged, and heads, including that of Daksha's, were chopped off. All the Lord of Destruction had left was the charred body of his wife. Her corpse on his shoulder, Shiva wandered the earth, his feet slowly dancing that dance of annihilation. Vishnu had to intervene. His spinning golden disc sliced Sati's body into fifty-two pieces, and Shiva finally stopped. His loss no longer had a token. For each of Sati's many pieces, believers built a temple, so Shiva could map his wife's remains. But her spirit, like him, stayed nomadic. I've seen it visit her devotees.

I was seven when my grandfather played a little game with me to test my resolve and measure my greed. For every minute I kept quiet, Nanu said he'd give me a rupee. Having already earned my week's allowance, I wanted my ten rupees to become twenty. My lips pursed, I sat cross-legged on a bed, peeved, yet determined. Suddenly, my mother burst into the room, caught hold of my hand and began running up the stairs of my grandfather's house. I was still counting the minutes on the watch Nanu had given me, but when I saw my mother nearly trip a second time, I had to ask her what the matter was. 'Sati Dadi is coming, and you're too young to see her,' she said.

Though upset by my mother's chronic censorship, I was also scared by her urgency. 'But how can a goddess come to Nanu's house?' I asked her. She was too breathless to speak. Leaving me in my cousins' room, all she said was, 'Keep the door locked and don't come out till I tell you.'

My heart racing and my palms sweaty, I lay under a blanket, waiting for an awful vision, petrified the world was about to change forever. I soon heard my grandmother shout. Nani-ma yelled like a banshee, and even though I was only a child, it didn't take long to understand she was not warding off a spirit. My loving nani, it became clear, had been possessed by one. I was sobbing when I opened the door for my mother, and the relief of her tight embrace has since been hard to forget. Many of my eager questions that night went unanswered. I was not told where the spirit of Sati had gone after she left my grandmother's body. I couldn't find out what would happen if it never left. Neither of my parents explained why Nani-ma had become so angry. Only after I'd exhausted him, did my father say he too would give me a rupee for every minute I was quiet. His two rupees wouldn't even buy me a samosa.

Four years later, when I was using defiance to flirt with adolescence, like many my age, I'd leave my mother exasperated with my apathy towards dipping maths scores. The one T-shirt of mine she loved I refused to wear. Her distress only grew when I stopped talking altogether. Worryingly, I didn't even need the incentive of that one rupee any more. We were again at my grandfather's house one night, when I saw my mother and her brother look flustered all of a sudden. They ran from one room to the next, and I thought I could recognize the panic I saw on my mother's face. She held my hand and said, 'Sati Dadi is here.' This was my first taste of déjà vu, and I expected another run up the stairs, but my mother, hoping to cure my obstinacy, took me to the room where my grandmother sat on a chair, her hair open and wild, her eyes bloodshot and her body all aquiver. Her screams were all prophecies. She said my cousin would soon get married. Her wedding, we knew, was imminent. That night, Sati predicted an already wealthy uncle would get rich, and she wanted my sister to study harder. The obviousness of these family forecasts was making me cynical, but a crippling fear didn't let me scoff.

I stood in a corner of the room, trying to fathom this absurd theatre of the divine. As my nani's arms started to flail, the members of my family began to prostrate before her in quick succession. She would bless each of them by pounding their backs with her fists. I still remember my grandfather going down on his knees and touching the feet of his wife. A decade later, I would attempt a short story where a man wakes up to discover that the woman he married was, in truth, a goddess. But that day, as a trembling eleven-year-old, I did not see any tenderness in his impromptu display of devotion. Crouched in front of my grandmother, my prayer to her was pathetic. 'Please don't hit me,' I whispered. The three blows on my back were forceful, though not excruciating. Sati was distinguished enough a guest for my grandmother's household to have exclusive tableware set aside for her. My aunt came sprinting in with a silver glass. The water did seem to cool my nani, and some ten minutes later, she sat spent and catatonic.

Even after having been in the presence of a bona fide goddess, I refused to speak. I sat in the back seat of our car, looking out of the window, sullen, still a little frightened.

My father felt it might be prudent to intervene. I thought he was being charitably chatty when he asked, 'Do you know where we come from, Bunshi?'

I was about to say 'the womb', but I chose to keep my lips sealed. 'We, your mother's family and ours, come from a little village in Rajasthan called Fatehpur, and in Rajasthan, people worship the goddess Sati. You know the story of Shiva and Sati, right?' I nodded. Glad to find his son well versed in matters essential and religious, he smiled and continued, 'So Sati, you know, set herself on fire after Shiva was insulted, but like her, there are other women who have done the same thing. Near Fatehpur, there were once two sisters who sat on a pyre with the body of their brother after he was killed. They started praying to the goddess Sati, and suddenly, they began to burn. Nobody had touched the pyre. Your grandmother worships the same goddess they did. And because her devotion is so great, Sati visits her sometimes.'

My mind in a flutter, I felt I had to speak. 'But what if Nani-ma too catches fire when Sati comes next?' My father sniggered before my mother shot him a livid glance. 'That's why they give her water,' he said.

My nani, I remember, was a matriarch. Her investment in the lives of her children and grandchildren would often come to border on obsession. Interested even in the stories her distant relatives and casual acquaintances had to tell, she would spend hours on the phone. She and my grandfather would bicker every morning, and he would then sit silently for a while, holding her hand. Her lungs had weakened with time, leaving her enfeebled, but her tenacity was formidable. Every other week, she would call to say she had made me French fries, and each time, she'd add, 'I know how you love them.' It was easy to forget the wildness of her possession. I had begun leaving the room when I saw her eyes redden, but on the day before I left for college, her hair voluntarily opened again. Chomping purposefully on my fries, I looked to see I was alone in the room with Sati.

Placing my chair in front of my grandmother, I began chanting 'I'm not scared' to myself. I had been curious about how my nani's identity would come to be replaced, and had once furiously scanned the Internet for an explanation. Spirit possession, I'd learnt, was invariably a symptom of trauma and psychological distress. And since the goddess had made a habit of casting her spell over some of my grand-aunts too, it was easy to infer that these visitations were in fact the manifestation of a mental affliction that was genetic. Having turned eighteen a few months ago, I had begun to take pride in my recently acquired pragmatism, but hearing my nani begin to speak loudly and somewhat incoherently, my powers of deduction were soon replaced by familial superstition.

This time, Sati did not hit my back with her fist. She gently caressed my hair and my face. 'I've given you your mind. Use it well,' she ordered. By the time I found her silver glass, she was bidding my grandmother goodbye. I made my nani sip the goddess's water. After she had regained some composure, she asked, 'Are you all right?' I nodded slowly. The silence we then sat in felt awkward.

After having spent almost a year in Falmouth, I had found a bench in a graveyard I liked to call mine. With half a dozen books stacked by my side, I would stop reading only to distract myself with cannabis and death. I had just finished smoking a joint and was trying to find archers and antelopes in the clouds when my grandmother called. Trying my best to mask my high and my newly acquired accent, I spoke to her about the weather, the new medicine our family doctor had put her on and the food I was eating. I didn't tell her I had bartered my vegetarianism for chicken Kievs, medium-rare steaks and spaghetti bolognese. With an authority that instantly made me feel both remorseful and nostalgic, my nani then asked, 'You haven't picked up any bad habits, have you?' My fingers still smelling of weed and my head in the clouds, I told her that all her grandchildren were born free of temptation. Leaving me swamped with guilt, she asked me to stay happy when she said goodbye.

I rolled myself a cigarette right after I had hung up. Long drags of cheap tobacco had always helped me rationalize my indiscretions, and on that autumnal afternoon, absolution didn't take long to come. My father once ate meat and my grandfather was a chain-smoker. Such imprudence she had forgiven before, and though the marijuana was seemingly more indefensible, I predictably found a precedent for it that was above all reproach. Sati, I told myself, the goddess my nani worshipped, must surely have had an attitude more permissive.

The Hindu pantheon offers its faithful a rare facility. With a multitude of gods and goddesses to choose from, devotees can let their personalities fashion their piety. In the household I grew up in, the path to spiritual plenitude was never formulaic. Finding comfort in incantation and fervour, my father had picked Durga. His mother, perennially maternal and nurturing, would spend her mornings bathing and dressing up an idol of baby Krishna. It was only my taciturn *bauji*, my sometimes-inconspicuous grandfather, who sought his salvation in the dispassion of Shiva. Sitting beside him, wanting to fit into the pocket of his starched white kurta, I would be fascinated by the props he'd collect on a tray to worship his beloved deity. Next to bowls of honey and sugar, there'd be a bright and fragrant pile of flowers— marigolds, roses and lotuses, picked carefully from our garden and Calcutta's lakes. Bauji let me dip my fingers into pastes of vermilion and sandalwood. He'd keep a towel to wipe my fingers clean. Even when bedecking the linga, he'd be patient with me and my curiosity.

In a tone I'd grow to consider exasperating, I once asked him, 'Why do we worship Nandi, Ganesha and Parvati when we worship Shiva? Why do we worship this snake?'

My grandfather was characteristically even in his response. 'Because you can't worship Shiva without worshipping his family,' he said. Seeing me caress two of the 108 trifoliate bael leaves he had painstakingly counted, he volunteered an explanation: 'Shiva has three eyes, and together they look like this leaf.'

I was hanging from his neck when I saw him reach for a cactoid fruit. He ran his fingers over its thorns. Without any regard for its sanctity, I asked contemptuously, 'What's *that*?'

My grandfather paused for a second. 'This is datura. It is poison for us, but Shiva loves it.' Emptying a packet of green powder on the linga, Bauji only smiled. 'Bhang helps Shiva forget that little boys like you ask too many questions.'

Years later, I'd tell myself I wasn't the first one to bring cannabis home. That day, I tried hard to wrap my arms around my grandfather, hugging him from behind.

When I snuggled on his belly, my bauji would tell me stories from the *Shiva Purana* with some delight. The god's penchant for bhang, however, was never mentioned. Cannabis, I later learnt, might have been an integral aspect of Shiva's symbology, but it was mostly omitted from his chronicles. Dissuading impressionable smokers from following Shiva's example, mythologists and clerics draw a careful distinction between intoxication and illumination. The renunciant Shiva, they argue, had little need for pleasure. For him, bhang obviates the world and its indulgences. I craved this precise transcendence when visiting Falmouth's graveyards, and while sitting cross-legged on its beaches. Marijuana would first make me paranoid, but as I grew accustomed to its influence, my senses discovered a sharpness that soon left me fearless. Shiva was prone to whimsy—he'd beheaded Ganesha, his son, Daksha, his father-in-law, Brahma, the Father—and like him, I grew impetuous, unworried by consequence.

Again smoking cannabis in 2012, again thinking of Shiva, I felt I needed to see a doctor when the abdominal pains I'd suffered for over a month turned savage. The diagnosis did not take long—'Your colon is inflamed. We call this ulcerative colitis. You have to be careful because there have been some cases where this has proved fatal.' Quitting my job a week later, I told my editor and colleagues I had been diagnosed with an illness that was terminal. The fiction was extravagant, but in my delusion, I had convinced myself of its veracity.

I had never felt more unafraid. I found a Shaivite abandon in the belief that there was no tomorrow. Wanting to re-enact 'The Last Supper', I threw a party for friends before I left Bombay. I made sure I had more wine than water. Walking around with bottles of alcohol all evening, I filled glasses with fanatical zeal. I gave away half my books—'I think I have read enough'—and then to further parade my lack of fear, I danced to my ridiculous playlist of Punjabi pop. That night, I offered my marijuana to Shiva before rolling it. I whispered into the ear of a friend, 'I want to be remembered as the guy who threw a mean party.'

Shiva himself, I'd soon write, is not an ideal guest at parties that insist on a dress code. A loincloth and tiger skin make for acceptable attire only on very few occasions, and a wedding is certainly not one of them. Shiva, unfortunately, didn't have much else in his wardrobe on the day he descended from Kailasa to marry Parvati. For the friends and sisters of the bride, the *baraat* is a thing of mirth and wonder. They expect a horse, a turban and formal regalia. The women of Himavat, it would follow, had reason to keel over. Shiva rode a bull. His entourage of deadly apparitions drank bhang from skulls, and the drums they beat foretold the arrival of death, not frolic. There was only ash, no finery. Disregarding that odd tradition of brides not seeing grooms until every member of her family has fawned over him, Parvati, indomitable and irate, decided she had to intervene. With her hands on her hips, a thin smile betraying her, she is imagined to have stood in front of Shiva and said, 'I'm not marrying you if you're going to come looking like that.' The world, she reminded him, demands that convention be followed. 'There's a time and place for everything.'

For Shiva, the world might be all too dispensable, but it is Parvati who makes him cognizant of its relevance. The goddess gives the Lord of Imbalances a structure of family, and it is in his role as husband and father that his chaos becomes comprehensible. Shiva was not an ascetic who had deigned to be a householder. He became the householder who was also sometimes an ascetic. It was in Parvati, the Puranas suggest, that Shiva felt he had again found his lost Sati.

Taking the flight from Bombay to Calcutta, closure seemed imminent but it had also begun to feel frustratingly elusive. Having landed, I was told my mother was waiting for me at the hospital. Still thinking I was a goblin in Shiva's retinue, I was intoxicated, unshaven, my eyes a fierce red. I had in my luggage an ashtray that was shaped like a skull. Walking through the corridors of an intensive care unit, I felt welcome. Death surely was release itself. I was, however, unprepared for the scene that awaited me in my nani's pink room. My emaciated grandmother lay on a hospital bed, tubes sticking out of her hands and neck, too tired to talk and too drained to be a vessel. Seeing me, my mother soon burst into tears. 'Her lungs are collapsing,' she told me. 'You should've told me,' I whispered, feeling suddenly sober.

As I saw my nani rapidly decline, I pulled the curtain on my own little drama. I needed to recognize my grandmother's suffering in order to forsake my theatrics and sentimentality. I sat by my nani's bed for hours on end. I counted the veins on her hand as I held it in mine. I grew obsessed with the levels of her oxygen concentrator and the eccentricity of her pulse.

The alleviation of pain, I told her doctor, should be a far more vital concern than prolonging her life. He nodded absent-mindedly, and then said, 'That's a fine line, son.' By the time my family had started talking in sobs and hushed whispers, I told my relatives I'd be getting married soon. 'That was her last wish,' I said. 'You are all obviously invited.'

Suddenness often gives death an inexplicable mystique. A mourning relative will say, 'I can't understand how she went so quickly,' and then the more philosophical acquaintance will feel compelled to add, 'That's the thing about death. It always comes unannounced.' In the case of my grandmother, however, the doctors came out to warn us she was breathing her last—'It's time to say your goodbyes.' Her few dozen relatives—sisters, brothers, sons, daughters, grandchildren, grand-nephews—all crowded her room, perhaps assuming she needed little space to breathe. More than her bodily presence, they would all come to miss her voice at the other end of a telephone. Involuntarily, I was pushed to my nani's side again, and I again came to hold her hand. My eyes were trained on the pulse meter that lay clipped to her finger. Seeing her heart rate slow considerably, I said quietly, 'I am Shiva, the God of Death, and I have come to collect your soul.' A minute or two later, when the oximeter had dropped to zero, my nani let out a sudden cry. The room gasped, and when I turned, I saw a hundred expectant eyes look at me. I could only shake my head.

Stricken and anxious, I shadowed my father for two consecutive days. I found comfort in the stories he would unexpectedly tell. Standing in my nani's garden, waiting to shoulder her corpse to the hearse, I told Pops, 'I felt Shiva had come to claim his Sati.' His interest piqued, he smiled and asked me to explain. 'I don't know what came over me, but when Nani-ma was passing away, I thought I was Shiva's proxy, taking the soul of his wife from the woman she would possess.' Unperturbed by my dramatic confession, my father, a devourer of all things mythological, put his hand on my shoulder to say, 'You've got your facts wrong, boy.' Making sure we were alone in the car on the way to the crematorium, he tried to iron out my frown. 'The Sati Dadi your grandmother worshipped, the Sati who she thought possessed her, is not quite the Sati who had married Shiva. The worship of your nani's Sati is fairly contentious.' Annoyed, I said, 'This is like telling me I was adopted. Besides, you're the one who told me they both worshipped the same goddess.'

My father was finding it hard to wipe off the smile that lingered on his face. 'We all worship the same goddess in the end, but that's the thing about Hinduism. It isn't set in stone. You can add any god or goddess to the pantheon, as and when you please. I could worship you tomorrow. All I need is your picture and a frame.' I couldn't help but chuckle at this point. 'I think you already have that.' Unusually loquacious, my father went on. 'What your nani worshipped was an idea. The scriptures describe a story that is incredible. Sati immolates herself because her father had insulted her husband. So, when women are burnt when their husbands or brothers die, that original myth is easily multiplied. The reason why Sati Dadi is not the same as Shiva's Sati is simple—Sati Dadi is a deity who is worshipped by families who inadvertently condone a practice that Sati's own immolation is a critique of. You don't die because you want to. You die because you have to. But if it helps ease your conscience, you can consider Sati Dadi an incarnation.'

The shame of misinterpretation stopped me from breaking into applause. My father had always been a raconteur, but his interpretation of religion had never seemed quite so eloquent. I confessed to him my guilt—'My belief, which you say is misplaced, has helped me imagine the most wondrous things, and my worry is not that I have mistaken regression for something it isn't. My worry is that I have offended the gods.' After staying silent for a few minutes, my father said slowly, 'Do you remember what Shiva did after he beheaded Brahma? To repent, he walked the earth with the Creator's skull stuck to his hand. When he went to Benares, the skull fell off on its own. So, you must do two things. Throw away that skull ashtray of yours, and then, go to Benares.'

6

Let the Great Web Spin

Three months after I had been diagnosed bipolar, I was miserable and sullen, but still haughty. By 2007, a number of my friends were on Facebook. Though social networking had not yet become a collective habit, it had already started to give its champions a novel ability to spy, stalk and speak. This new stage, I felt, was already too crowded. Alone in my Chennai flat, feeling both my body and mind grow heavy, I told a friend on the phone, 'My fingers were trembling so terribly today, I dropped my cup of coffee on a colleague's keyboard. That isn't even the worst part. The worst part is the isolation. I have nowhere to go and no one to meet.' I sounded pathetic and I feared I had begun to tire her with my despair.

'It's time you got over yourself and joined Facebook,' she said. 'You couldn't have a more effortless experience. Everyone you like is in one place. You can start as many conversations as you want without leaving your room. It comes customized for depressives, really.'

On 28 September 2007, I finally succumbed, and my capitulation was predictably met with queries and exclamation

125

marks. 'Never thought I'd find you here!' said a friend, while another laughed, 'You fell into the Facebook trap!' An ex-lover asked, 'What's this out-of-character behaviour?' and the unanimous gasp of surprise was succinctly summed up by the reaction of one acquaintance—'Hey there . . . social networking . . . u???' It was a dear friend from Falmouth who proved the most prophetic. 'Ho, ho, ho, you'll regret this, maybe,' he typed. Every such message, I felt, demanded a reply, and as dialogue began to feel obligatory, I lost all yearning for it. Facebook, it turned out, offered my depression very little solace. My friends were all happier than me, their humour was more witty and their pictures more gleeful. Having aimlessly scrolled down the walls of my acquaintances for two weeks, I then stayed away from social media for the next fifteen months. My bipolarity had made me a victim and I believed my need for interaction was not worth the exhibition.

When I failed to resurrect my journalistic career in Chennai and Bombay, I moved to Brighton in the September of 2008 for my master's degree. Living in a house with ten other international students, my despondency was soon replaced by a welcome bounce. My Facebook wall, which had been bare enough for me to be called the 'master of silence', was suddenly alive. My housemates had posted photos of me with whisky bottles, cigarettes and women who were unattainable. I had found rescue in university life, and the fun I was having was being carefully catalogued. When a former colleague commented that parties at Sussex were 'seemingly never-ending', I patted myself on the back. 'I do have a life!' The exuberance I discovered soon made me forget my torment.

Disregarding the instructions my psychiatrist had repeated before I left—'You must sleep for eight hours a day'—I used coffee, marijuana, Sigmund Freud and J.M. Coetzee to stay up for seven nights in a row. Every day, I would visit my college library to exchange one haul of books for another. My room smelt like an ashtray. The imminent deadline for the submission of two essays was my justification for the insomnia I manufactured. The world, meanwhile, had changed.

On 20 January 2009, a day after I had sprinted down the campus to smuggle my essays in at the last minute, Barack Obama was sworn in as President of the United States. The moment was significant enough for the University of Sussex to celebrate, but it was strangely a call from my nani that made the event dangerously critical. 'I was seeing this new President Obama on TV, and I thought it was you talking.' In an instant, the effervescence I felt turned itself into a sinister grandeur. I grew obsessed with the idea that I was ordained for eminence.

I was manic when I updated my Facebook status for the very first time. 'Shreevatsa Nevatia,' I wrote, 'is waiting for the next Obama,' and then to disguise my pomp, I wondered if Obama would have sex that night. In a few minutes, people began talking back, and the sense of connectedness I had begun to relish became exaggerated and literal. Unaccustomed to the precariousness of a Facebook user's attention, I felt I'd captivated my audience. As an undergraduate, I had a crush on a senior who had once made me dance for her amusement. I was thrilled when I saw her engage with my posts. When she contemptuously mentioned Shakira's performance at Obama's inauguration, I reminded her that Gabriel García Márquez's profile of the singer was glowing and delightful. When she mentioned Bono, I immediately thought of Rushdie. I knew they were friends. Seeing she had typed the word 'cool', I ranted about Camus smoking a cigarette, and my unfiltered responses soon became far-fetched and pretentious.

I had written my essays in a state of mild euphoria, and over that sleepless week, I was continuously surprised by how malleable language had begun to seem. Words which were once remote miraculously made themselves available. Academic jargon was easy to unpack, and authenticity was mine to claim. Without the structure of formal assignments, however, my thoughts grew unruly, racing from one suggestion to the next. Facebook was where I did all my writing. I had no new ideas to trumpet and no cleverness to boast of. I could only map the six degrees that separated me from the world, and it was this ability to connect disparate dots that made my mania momentous. On Facebook, my free association proved more tyrannical than therapeutic. I expected my audience to keep up. Initially flirtatious, the exchange of messages with my college senior soon came to be tinged with an aggressive unease. Exhausted by my incoherence, she said, 'Difference of opinion this. Let's leave it at that.' I was being sardonic when I replied, 'And I am stunned by your unfailing wit.' Obviously irate, she added, 'Talk in English, or don't talk.' Silence, for me, was not an option, so I then sent her six messages in quick succession.

In 2007, suffering my first bout of mania, I had perilously perched on a windowsill to play imaginary chess with my best friend. Drawing squares with my finger on the marble and moving an imaginary pawn down the makeshift board, I had told Natty, 'Sports are for teams, but games are meant for two. It's not the winning that counts, it's the playing. And to be able to play, I need you.' I did not need Natty to witness my mania. I simply needed him to participate in it.

A year and a half later, loneliness had again become oppressive, and it was in Facebook's invented community of ready listeners that I found a cure for my solitude. I wasn't just being nostalgic for Natty's amity when I typed that I wanted someone to teach me how to play chess. I wanted someone in my room, sitting opposite me, laughing at my puns, wowed by my repartee. When I said that I wanted 'to go watch *Slumdog Millionaire*', I desperately hoped an acquaintance would say they would go to the cinema with me. My mania had made me needy. I wanted acknowledgement and applause. Sadly, I'd met a rather tough crowd.

The enlightenment I had stumbled upon was laughably facile. I felt messianic not because everything I saw was illuminated. I had just the one grand idea—everything is linked. Language soon became the strand that tied together the universe and its awareness. To demonstrate the patterns words create, I began writing ridiculous free verse in response to the increasingly annoyed messages of friends—'Slowness, so sweet I tell you. / Like honey. / OK, maybe Demerara. / Chocolate for sure though.' Wanting to be anointed, I proposed that 'we all should have a Facebook party'. I was admittedly being disingenuous when I said guests should bring piñatas and balloons. What I really wanted was some sandalwood, a crown, a procession. Expectedly, none of my hare-brained plans had any takers, so I went off in a sulk, announcing I was going to look up 'pejorative' in the dictionary. In a few minutes, I had returned to say I was 'going to leave the dictionary after having gotten carried away a little'.

Updating my status every five minutes, I was not yet aware that I had inadvertently taken over the timelines and newsfeeds of almost everyone who had become part of my friends list. Simmi, my housemate and confidante, opened the door to my room at six in the morning one day and said, 'I see Finnegan has been awake all night.' She came and sat next to me on my bed, put her arm around my shoulder and asked, 'Are you all right, Shev?' Resting my head against hers, I said, 'Never been better, but I don't think anyone gets it.' She was intent on soothing my tumult. 'Some of us do, but we're equally concerned about you. You have not slept in days, and that cannot be good for that pretty head of yours. Please rest.'

Simmi pointed to a message a childhood friend had posted and read aloud, 'Shreevatsa must realise that every thought he has and everything he does need not be articulated through Facebook status changes. And he should go to bed.' As I broke into a chuckle, Simmi too laughed helplessly. 'You need to explain to me what is going on,' she demanded. 'I've never felt freer, Sim. It's like pain doesn't matter any more, and my mind feels like it has realized what it had always wanted to. It has no need for sleep, no need to rest.' Simmi, an Indo-Canadian postgraduate student, did not look incredulous. She spoke as if she understood. 'And you feel you have to tell the world what you know?' I was quick to reply: 'What's the point of knowledge if it cannot be shared?' Simmi smacked me on the head and countered, 'You might be feeling all Buddha about yourself, but the world thinks you are on drugs. I hope you know that.' I smiled. 'I read that, and quite honestly, some drugs would be nice at this point.' She frowned. 'I'm giving you another two hours to spread the word. After that I'm taking you out for breakfast.' Once she had left the room, I felt soaked with warmth. 'Shreevatsa Nevatia is learning how to travel light,' I typed. I did feel free of baggage, yes, but more worryingly, I had begun to think I could tame the velocity of my hurtling mind.

As I constantly referred to myself in the third person, my already rambling posts came to seem even more psychotic. When a former colleague called to say, 'You sound like a man possessed in your posts,' I did not stop to consider the dissonance of my grammar. I instead dismissed him with some disdain, saying, 'I'm afraid exorcisms have stopped being carried out on the phone.'

Minutes later, I calmed myself enough to see some merit in his reason. No longer was I 'Shreevatsa Nevatia'. Shreevatsa was someone I was inventing as I went along. By distancing myself from the words I was compulsively broadcasting, I decided I had absolved myself of responsibility and excess. The abandon I then began to feel was unbridled. The unseemly update—'Shreevatsa Nevatia can't wait to have sex with Kate Winslet'—came a short while after I had asked if anyone wanted to swap passwords and edit the other's profile. Even in the throes of mania, I found it hackneyed to think we construct our virtual identities, but while creating an alter ego, a second Shreevatsa, I wanted another to bring me a change.

After fifteen hours of my madness having become a parade of over fifty status updates, Facebook fell quiet. When

I alluded to Britney Spears's 'Hit me baby one more time', a classmate wrote on my wall, 'I'm more than willing to give someone a good beating right now.' The world had not unified to proclaim my advent and it did not laud my performance. It was inexplicably irritated by my blathering. Threatening to sign off, I grovelled for approval. 'Shreevatsa Nevatia,' I wrote, 'is now convinced he has so bored his audience, he wants to retire.' No one wanted to follow me to Tintern Abbey and no one wanted to sing Led Zeppelin for my amusement. My disappointment now became a tantrum. Minutes before Simmi returned to bang the lid of my laptop shut, I had typed, 'No more of this. Thank you for Facebooking. A fat load of good all you people have done me . . . Adios.'

Walking to the cafe where she worked, Simmi put her arm through mine and asked, 'How does a man who abhorred Facebook become its most visible star in just one night?' I was still despondent. 'I think you need fans to be a star.' She raised her hand and held out two fingers in a manner I had come to know as both hip-hop and characteristic. 'That's your problem. You think you don't have any and yet the house phone won't stop ringing. There are so many people who love you.' Crotchety and obstinate, I snapped, 'You must know that their concern is really just a form of control.' Simmi held me tighter. 'They're all far away, Shev. If you care for someone, you have the right to worry.' By ten in the morning, all my friends from Brighton to Bombay had woken up to see the manic trail I had left on their Facebook walls. Seeing I was finally offline, their exasperation then turned to panic. As I ate my eggs and drank my coffee, Simmi kept leaving the table to answer her phone, which rang stubbornly. When I stepped outside to smoke my cigarette, I could see her pacing down the street, her face frozen with consternation. When she reached for my lighter, her hands shivered in the cold. 'Shev, your shenanigans have a downside. You're going to have to come with me to the doctor. You need to trust me. I will be with you. I will not let anything happen to you.' I felt unexpectedly pliant.

In 2009, neither Simmi nor I had a smartphone that would have helped me compute the number of likes my posts had received or the number of comments they had spurred. But I was distracted anyway. As we waited for Dr Donelson in the waiting room of a private clinic, Simmi tried to hold my promiscuous attention with talk of our essays and my fiction. 'I will never forgive you if you give up on your writing,' she said. My response left her discernibly confounded. 'If I had to be reincarnated, I'd like to be born as a ladyboy in Bangkok.'

When the receptionist announced my name, I straightened my shirt and smoothed my stubble. Simmi kept her promise. She came inside with me. The understated chamber of Dr Donelson and his sombre countenance tacitly made a demand for logic. I told him, 'In 2007, a psychiatrist in Bombay, a quack by all standards, diagnosed me bipolar. I have been on lithium and Depakote ever since. It's only when I went off these to write my essays that I was able to feel some levity again.'

I confessed to him that I hadn't slept in over a week, 'But I have never really felt more alive or awake in my life.' After I had rambled on for a while longer, the bearded psychotherapist asked if he could speak to Simmi alone for a minute or two. 'He is manic,' he told her, 'but what he

sorely needs at this point is sleep.' Seeing that Simmi did
not walk out with a prescription, I felt jubilant to have not
been incarcerated. I later exclaimed, 'Sim, no straitjacket for
me no more!' Her smile was forlorn. 'I'll be taking away your
computer, mister.'

Walking down the streets of Brighton, feeling the
warmth of the winter sun on my face, certain that I was
only being observed and not followed, I embraced my
expansiveness. Dragging her into a bookshop, I saw Simmi's
surprise metamorphose into shock when I told a salesman,
'Please choose for me books worth two hundred pounds.
I'll buy anything you recommend. I've been reading a lot
of trash on Facebook. I need something more nourishing.'
For the next hour, though, I treated literature in the exact
manner I'd recently devised for online prattle. When the
salesman showed me a copy of Flannery O'Connor's *The
Complete Stories* and pointed to 'A Good Man Is Hard to
Find', I told him, 'I should know. It took me twenty-six years
to find myself.' Stopping to consider Jayne Anne Phillips's
MotherKind, I turned to Simmi and quipped, 'I really would
not have become who I am if my mothers hadn't been so kind.'
As I turned pages of books I'd never heard of, I told myself
that any line I'd stop at would offer up a key to the universe.
Flipping through *2666*, I thought I had discovered a prophet
in Roberto Bolaño. I demanded the store bring me a pencil
when I chanced upon two sentences that seemed wonderfully
felicitous: 'So everything lets us down, including curiosity and
honesty and what we love best. Yes, said the voice, but cheer
up, it's fun in the end.' Seeing me buy eighteen books, Simmi
could only say, 'Facebook is cheaper.'

Having helped carry my haul across the city, Simmi left me in my room with the instruction, 'You be good now. I mean it.' I refused to obey and I soon took to Facebook to announce my book-shopping at Waterstones. Within minutes I received a call from a hysterical friend in Delhi. She shouted, 'Stop annoying the world with your status updates. You are becoming an imposition. I hope you know that.' I shouted back, 'Then why don't you and everyone else block me. That would be simpler, right?' While talking, I had already typed out my next post: 'Shreevatsa Nevatia is not going to stop updating his status . . . You have a choice . . . A very good one . . . Make it.'

Anger tires you faster than ecstasy. I had finally dozed off when I heard someone knocking on my door. Strangely, I wasn't surprised to see Mallika, my anxious and perturbed ex-girlfriend, standing on the other side. Also in Britain as a postgraduate student now, Mallika had caught the next train when my interminable social networking had made my mania common knowledge.

I met her with fury. 'Who sent you here?' I demanded. 'No one did. I just wanted to come see you. I can do that, can't I?' The calm her voice had feigned would prove fragile. I asked, 'You mean to say that none of the people who have been calling me have called you?' She replied with some trepidation, 'We're friends. We call each other. You're not okay. We just want to make sure you are.' I stormed back into my room and seeing her stand in its corner, I decided to assault her timidity. 'I'm sick and tired of this mollycoddling. There's nothing wrong with me. There never was. I do not need you and I certainly do not need all this care.'

When I was fighting with the world, even my kindest benefactor was an adversary. Grabbing my passport, wallet and *2666*, I glared at Mallika and said, 'You should never have come here.' Before leaving the house, I started up my laptop one last time. I logged back into Facebook and typed, this time in first person—'I forgot to say to my invisible audience . . . Et tu . . . The show is now over.'

Halfway down the street, I heard Simmi yell, 'And where do you think you're going?' My indignation had given way to despair. 'Back to India, to show the world I'm fine.' She laughed. 'I'm coming with. Not to Delhi, but at least till Heathrow. Oh, and if you are going back, I'm going to be taking your computer, this time for keeps.'

On the train, I asked Simmi for her iPod. 'I need something to remember you by,' I told her. In London, she walked me to my terminal and hugged me tight again. 'Don't do anything I wouldn't,' she warned. A day later, strapped to a hospital bed in Delhi, I would wake up and scream, 'Simmi has my laptop. She'll set me free. Just you wait. She will come for me.'

~

The news came early on 6 April 2010. In an attack that was described as 'brazen' and a 'massacre', over two hundred Maoist guerrillas had ambushed and killed seventy-six personnel of the Central Reserve Police Force. In Chhattisgarh's Dantewada, wrote an overwrought reporter, 'a nation was at war with itself'. P. Chidambaram, who was then India's home minister, was more inexplicit. 'Something has gone very wrong,' he said.

In the Delhi offices of the national magazine where I worked, journalists were convinced the Maoists had not just disturbed the status quo, they had shredded it. My editor pulled me aside to say, 'They're bringing back the bodies of the jawans tomorrow. You have to go to Uttar Pradesh in the morning and meet the grieving families. Just capture the mood. You don't have much time.' He glowered at me when I said, 'Someone really should have told the jawans that.'

I stayed as wilful when I skipped my lithium later that night. It had been a while since I had woken up at four.

Wired on coffee and cigarettes, I was again thinking of Shiva when I saw Fakhruddin Khan fall on the grave of his twenty-nine-year-old son, Khalil. 'We have nothing, we have no land. Khalil was the only support I had. Whatever happens has already been written by God,' he cried.

For me, even his fatalism was a stimulant. At the home of Narendra Kumar, the grief was louder. Women wailed in a circle and beat their chests. A nine-month-old baby whimpered noisily. Only Shridhan Singh, the father, was quiet. 'I am not crying like them, but my soul is,' he finally said. As I stayed up to file my report that night, my mania graduated from my distress, not my elation. The brutality of violence and its appeal monopolized my imagination. I theorized death with a renewed obsession. I wanted to be unafraid.

My Facebook updates had turned tentative after I had acknowledged that in January 2009, I had suffered what a friend called a 'sorry social media meltdown'. Signing into the website, I had begun to feel more scrutinized than entertained. Thirteen months later, my wall saw very little activity. With pictures and impulsive posts, my girlfriend made several attempts to resurrect my virtual self, but my few status messages remained clumsy and apologetic—'Lumpen— That's my word, I just found it. That's me!' On 11 April, however, my courage was restored. I wanted to tell the world I had found the end to suffering, that there was no afterlife, and that the state both curbed and necessitated violence. Though unoriginal, these thoughts seemed urgent. Yet, when faced with the keyboard, wanting to see Facebook come alive again, I was paralysed. Social networking, I believed, needed you to be whimsical and droll to be popular. Any talk of death would surely make me a grim outcast. And I wanted to wage war, but I also wanted to be liked. It was in the lyrics of a White Stripes song—'Seven Nation Army'—that I found my update. 'Shreevatsa Nevatia,' I typed, 'is trying to wonder which seven nations he should choose for his seven nation army.' No one thought I was out for revenge. It is not a surprise, no one responded.

The lack of approval had left me downcast, but I didn't remain dispirited for very long. The soapbox Facebook allowed me to climb proved more emancipating than the endorsement of its users. A single status update had liberated me from the torment of the tragedy in Dantewada, and it had again given my incipient mania the consolation of a voice.

Though less persistent, my posts over the next few days were baffling. The sound of words had again started to matter more than their meaning. I warned that one should always avoid writers—'Never get too close, they are all pen pricks.' I desperately wanted someone to laugh when I said I felt 'Mondayne' on a Thursday. I suggested that the new form of communication I had invented be called 'Cryptique', a mix of 'cryptic, critic and mystique'. Suddenly aware of perception and consequence, I added, 'These pretentious types should all be shot.' Disillusioned by the promise of perpetual engagement Facebook made, I confessed I was impatient. I wanted someone to come up and say, 'Knock, knock.'

To those who knew me well, my hectic social networking was obviously a symptom. I cried 'déjà vu' when Rito, a dear friend from Calcutta, appeared at my door, saying, 'I logged on to Facebook. I had to take the next flight.' I banged the door shut in his face. I shouted, 'And you're here to shoot the messenger, are you?'

For journalists, the freedom of speech is a slippery grail they covet and fiercely protect. As Rito spent the hot April night on my terrace, I practised my case against censorship, and I called my unsuspecting parents long past midnight to ask, 'Why have you sent someone to arrest me? I haven't broken any law.'

Two days later, however, I was softened by Rito's conviviality and empathy. I found myself overwhelmed by remorse. I took the flight home with him. Though I swallowed my lithium, I remained nostalgic for manic facility.

A month later, I found myself oscillating between depression and euphoria. I did long for a hug when I typed, 'Someone should put me to rest. Now would be nice,' but I equally wished someone would drop by to slit my throat.

Eventually chastened and repentant, I strived to make my Facebook profile inconspicuous over the next two years. In delicately worded emails, I was informed that my social networking would be monitored. I was a representative of the newspapers where I worked, and prying HR departments would perhaps not take kindly to posts that sometimes bordered on inappropriate and rude. Rather than considering such interventions Orwellian, I thought them fortuitous. Only ever posting the pieces and reports I had written and edited, I found self-promotion was more prudent than self-exposure. A colleague once sidled up to say, 'You're all work and no play, man.' I sounded unintentionally plaintive when I replied, 'That's only because I have been sent off too many times.'

By 2013, though, Facebook had changed in a manner that was significant, yet imperceptible. I didn't need language to join the disparate dots of my mania. To circumvent the surveillance of my office and that of intelligence agencies who I was convinced were following me, I posted a few dozen stills from films to archive my every mood. Playing the reporter Joe Wershba in George Clooney's *Good Night, and Good Luck*, Robert Downey Jr personified the kind of dogged journalistic integrity I felt I had come to embody. An actor in *Sin City* looked suitably indignant, and when I changed my cover photo to a shot of Christopher Plummer singing 'Edelweiss' in *The Sound of Music*, I silently yearned for the sufficiency of my grandmother's lullabies.

Facebook gave the sentimentality of my mania a proxy, and minutes before I was carried away to a mental institution, I had pinned to my wall a still from *Fight Club*. Brad Pitt, Edward Norton's invented counterpart, stands with his hair dishevelled, a cigarette hanging from his lips, and blood trickling down his bare body. As a caption, I settled on a quote from Dostoevsky's *The Double*: 'A man's perishing here, a man's vanishing from his own sight here, and can't control himself—what sort of wedding can there be!' I was stupefied when a therapist soon pointed to the image as proof of my violence and manic cognizance.

~

Both in my depression and my madness, I had found it hard to answer the question 'How to be alone?' I thought it essential to remind myself that my desire for communication and connectedness was in fact a manic predilection. It seemed odd that by 2016, all my friends, colleagues and relatives also felt that their whimsy and vanity needed an audience. They had all signed up on Facebook and Twitter. Like me, they were all desperate for that sometimes-elusive Facebook 'like', and like me, they all wondered why their Twitter followers were ever so reluctant to retweet their stray thoughts and their writing. 'The world has gone bipolar,' I once told my analyst. 'But not everyone obsesses about their every online interaction,' she laughed. My deductions, I had to confess, were simplistic.

Unlike Facebook, where affinity and affection ensured token engagement, Twitter proved a more unfriendly beast. Followers weren't as kind as friends. Its frenzied chaos served well the popular, the dramatic and the abrasive. I, however, found the invented familiarity of strangers clumsy, and I found impossible the brevity of the 140 characters Twitter stipulated. Twitter moved too quickly, and despite my few earnest efforts, I couldn't keep up. I only ever used the platform to advertise my journalism and that of my colleagues. On 23 January, though, I sat in my Bombay flat, reading seven books all at the same time, seeing language become porous and my mind grow nimble. Even my Twitter feed had suddenly transformed into a source of felicity.

My manic self refuses to believe in coincidence, so when I saw a tweet by Margaret Atwood that night, my faith in providence was affirmed. 'Thrilled to be @JaipurLitFest #India! Tweet Qs now, hash #MargaretAtwood, will answer tomorrow, 24th, 5pm,' she had written. One of the books that lay open on my bed was a review copy of Atwood's *The Heart Goes Last*. I remembered being enchanted by Atwood when I had read *The Blind Assassin* in my mid-twenties, and in a moment of rare lightness, I found a fittingly frivolous question to put to the author—'My very silly question—Was the blind assassin wearing a blindfold? #MargaretAtwood.' Though I was already delirious, I did not expect Atwood to answer. Twitter, I believed, had little time for my playfulness. Atwood thankfully did. She tweeted back at the promised hour—'Nope. Actually blind. (In the story within the story.) As Justice, however: definitely!' My hysteria was as inordinate as my laughter. I thanked Atwood profusely, not just for her reply, but for every word she had ever written. She went on to other questions.

Like the boy who has just convinced his favourite cricketer to sign his shirt, my step in the next few days found a new swagger. To friends, I admitted that for the first time in eight years, I had truly been surprised by social media and the remarkable possibilities of contact it facilitated. Rather than dismiss my exchange with the Booker-winning Atwood as fantastic and flippant, I started considering it pivotal and life-changing. Stephen Fry too had liked one of my tweets, and after I had gotten embroiled in my first Twitter spat, calling @UserDarth 'Daft Vader', I told a college friend I had impulsively decided to meet, 'This Twitter thing makes me feel I have finally arrived.' Parking her car, Ameera said, 'You certainly cannot say that until you're on Instagram.' She grabbed my phone. Having created my account in a matter of minutes, she found on my phone a picture my mother had recently taken of my sister and me. 'This sort of thing really works,' Ameera chuckled. 'It's not a vain selfie, and it shows you're a family guy.'

I confessed to Ameera I was a terrible photographer. 'My hands shake all the time.' She ran her nails through her hair and said consolingly, 'Here, take a picture of me. Your phone will fix that tremble.' Looking at the picture of hers I had just clicked, I told her, 'You look lovely, but the lighting is all wrong.' She peered over my shoulder. 'You will not post that. My nose looks much bigger than it actually is, but what you don't need to worry about are things like light and angles. You just need to embrace the ordinary. That's the point of this.' Ameera was full of tips that night. Gliding her fingers across pictures she had posted, she advised, 'It isn't always your picture that tells a story. You're a journalist, so you should know how to give a good caption. But more importantly, your hashtag is your headline. You want words that someone will want to use, words they'll remember.'

My parents live on the thirteenth floor of a high-rise in Calcutta, and I have invariably gone home to recover from my mania and also to survive it. By the February of 2016, I had again quit my job on a whim, my manner had again become gregarious, and my speech zippy. Calcutta brought transient comfort, but also a bedroom window and balcony that provided perfect frames for my initial Instagram flirtations. Unlike Facebook posts, Instagram pictures, I was convinced, could never betray the exaggerations of my mind. I took pictures of the city in the morning and invoked E.M. Forster in my hashtag—'#TheRoomWithAView'. Ameera was impressed by a caption I'd given my picture of the Calcutta skyline at dusk. 'Sun. Set. Match,' she repeated. 'It's clever.' At night, '#MinimumCity' seemed like an appropriate tag, and Ameera was again forced to comment, 'Your theme certainly has variations, but you really do need to leave that window now.'

Growing up, I came to realize that thirteenth-floor apartments leave you unafraid of heights. Standing by that very window I had now taken to recording obsessively, I had spent a considerable part of my adolescence asking questions that were admittedly morbid. If I were to throw myself down, would I fall head first? Would my skull make a sound when it cracked? How quickly would gravity act? If I fell on a car, would I bounce off it or would I shatter its windscreen? Would my picture make it to the papers? Years later, Instagram helped me choreograph suicide. I found on my shelves a copy of Richard Crasta's *The Killing of an Author* and I carefully placed it on the windowsill. Training my camera on the book's title and the drop below, I thought of my caption—'And then she said, Jump!' Thirteen friends liked the image, two commented, and one called to say, 'Stop with all this attention-seeking.' I laughed. 'As far as suicide notes go, this would've been oh so original, no?'

On 23 February, I posted a selfie on Instagram that only helped confirm a collective realization. My darkness had fast started losing its humour. Holding my phone in my left hand, the afternoon light of a late winter falling on my face, I clicked a picture of myself that was intended to be my declaration of purpose. Wearing headphones, a rosary around my wrist, I held between my teeth a lighter and I set it aflame with the index finger of my right hand. 'That's right!' I exclaimed. 'This country makes me want to breathe fire. I am done though. It's getting bloody hot in here.' Mania has a habit of leaving you in a state of constant departure, but I was not just leaving that day. I believed I was being exiled. Unlike the spontaneous rage that friends and acquaintances expressed on social media, mine was choreographed, and as a consequence, it was more dramatic.

Already protesting hierarchy, I took easily to defending dissent when the now-famous four students of Jawaharlal Nehru University were arrested by the Delhi police in mid-February. Their opposition to the hanging of a Kashmiri separatist was one I could readily endorse. Accused of shouting anti-India slogans, these students had been charged with sedition, and like the majority of India's liberal class, I had begun using words like 'fascistic' and 'totalitarian' when describing the high-handedness of the country's right-wing BJP government. As a journalist, I had prized stoicism and political neutrality, but unemployed and manic, I found social media activism was better suited to the revolution I'd joined and wished to lead. I tagged the prime minister and his cabinet in tweets that were deliberately inflammatory. Convinced my every online remark was being observed, I was theatrically provocative when I called members of the BJP a 'bunch of godless thugs' and its supporters a pack of 'scoundrels'. On 28 February, I took to Facebook fifty-six times. I mused about

God, Salinger and the Oscars, but found it hard to altogether forsake my outrage. My online aggression spilt over. I accused my parents of corruption and my friends of apathy. Later that night, when a bouncer led me to an ambulance, I asked him, 'Did Narendra Modi send you? Does he enjoy watching me?'

Scattered on various social networking platforms, the evidence of my excess is too substantial to delete entirely and it is too stark to forget. Having been documented as virtual history, my mania also has anniversaries Facebook prompts me to share.

Every 21 January, it reminds me I was once 'waiting for the next Obama'. On 29 May, it embarrasses me with a notification that in 2010, Shreevatsa Nevatia had 'just sold his youth to the devil in exchange for a woman who sings endless soul'.

I wait for my 19 February memory, however. On that day in 2016, I stole a cartoon from a friend's wall. Sitting in his leather chair, a psychoanalyst asks his client on the couch, 'Do any of your relatives suffer from mental illness?' His client looks exasperated when she says, 'No . . . They all seem to enjoy it.' No one acknowledged that post. I've found comfort in thinking no one was listening.

7

Missing the Deadline

In November 2015, waiting to interview Deepika Padukone and Ranbir Kapoor, I stood in the lobby of a Bombay luxury hotel, surrounded by mirrors. My reflection did not flatter or assure me. In the five months since I had moved to the city, I had gained three kilos. I felt obese. To cover my belly, I hadn't tucked my shirt in. My stubble had grown scraggy. Though I was always fated to bald, the cocktail of drugs I'd been prescribed had only hastened that inevitable recession.

When I called my sister to tell her I was about to meet her two favourite stars, she first asked, 'What are you wearing?' The call was something of a ritual. Demanding an exhaustive account of my few encounters with film celebrities, she'd once said to me, 'It is the only time I feel like living vicariously through you.' My mania often gave my sister and me a lot to talk about. We would reminisce and laugh. She'd be protective and comforting. 'I think you like to call me only when you're losing it,' she had said. She was not wrong. In times more lucid, I found her vigilance overbearing.

As a child, I would devour my sister's glossy movie magazines for their steamy pictures, but as a teenager, I took to reading the interviews of actors with some avidity. I was fascinated by a very obvious idea—emotions like ecstasy, pain, ennui, anger and bemusement only had to be performed for them to be real. To fool audiences, you only had to entertain them. Though a string of auditions for school plays had proven I was a terrible actor, I was never dissuaded. In order to guarantee the affection of my parents, teachers, friends and my sister, I simply had to tell them the few things they each wanted to hear. Mania, I later found, would hand me an already written script. Always the protagonist, I would also at times play the superhero. I would save the world and leave it confounded with my ability. I'd send it rolling in the aisles with my puns. The depression that inevitably followed sought a more laborious performance.

When you're manic, you do everything to avert the end of the world, but when depressed, the pieces of your apocalypse prove too heavy to pick up. Depression seldom gives your hopelessness a narrative, and without a story to tell, your improvisations, you find, are as awkward as the smiles you manufacture. It becomes hard not to ham your way through the drama of despair. Deepika Padukone, I assumed, knew this well. Earlier that year, in March, I had seen the actor break down on television while detailing her struggle with depression. 'I woke up feeling directionless, I didn't know where to go, I didn't know what to do and I had these bouts of feeling so low that I would just start crying at the drop of a hat,' she had said. Strangely, one of India's biggest stars had become relatable only after she confessed that she'd often escape to her vanity van to sob helplessly. It had been estimated that 36 per cent of the country was afflicted with depression, and Padukone was not just a mascot, she had become our spokesperson. When depressed, Padukone was filming *Happy New Year*, a goofball comedy, and I desperately wanted to ask her the most hackneyed of all journalistic questions—'So, how did that feel?' My sister was not impressed when she heard of my intent. 'Listen to me and keep it light,' she warned.

Film stars were hard to interview, as I had confessed to her once. Their celebrity invariably punctured my journalistic cool, and even though my questions never pandered, I feared my manner did. Regrettably, they also had the habit of making you wait. I looked at my watch to see that my interview had already been delayed by an hour and a half. But I found I could forgive Ranbir Kapoor and Deepika Padukone their lack of punctuality. Actors can, of course, easily get carried away. They don't always know when to stop. Suffering from what can perhaps be termed an opulence of beauty, Padukone, for instance, had spent a fair part of her early career acting in films that each reduced her to a pretty face. It was only when her characters became vulnerable to hurt and bruises, when they started having sex out of wedlock, that she confirmed her reliability as a performer. She was again doing a film with Kapoor, her ex, with whom her relationship had been as public as her break-up. The questionnaire I'd recently printed had typed itself.

Finally ushered into a room the size of a school playground and with an obvious paucity of furniture, I found Deepika Padukone sitting on one of the room's two chairs, getting her make-up touched up. Her stature and skin both seemed impossibly perfect. There was some solace in the idea that beauty, even Padukone's, needed to be crafted.

Half-sprawled on a lush white couch next to her, Ranbir Kapoor fiddled with his phone. His stardom, earned but also inherited, allowed him his mild disinterest. I waited to be acknowledged.

Padukone was apologetic. 'You must have been standing outside for quite some time,' she said. Disarmed by her unexpected kindness, I had to coax myself to stay provocative. 'How is it that you, Ranbir, are always coming of age in the films you do with Deepika? And Deepika, how do you always manage to be such a rock?'

Padukone didn't smile. In a tone that was almost stern, she said, 'I'd like to believe that every film has its own journey; that every director is trying to express something very different.' Kapoor soon softened to describe his youth as 'mediocre', and he and Padukone were both forgiving when answering the question, 'Isn't it strange to be performing love with someone you'd once practised all its rituals with?' Kapoor laughed. 'We're not love gurus,' he said.

Even though Padukone had made her depression public and talked about it with great candour, it took me half an hour to bring up the subject. Despair, I had learnt, is prone to relapse, and recollections often exaggerate one's susceptibility. Just talking about it can be enough. In order to reduce my guilt about having to ask, I chose to preface my question with an apology. 'Having grappled with depression for a while myself,' I had started saying when Padukone stopped me. She sounded concerned when she asked, 'You've suffered depression too?'

I wasn't prepared for her sincerity. 'Yes, for as long as I can remember.' Inexplicably, she smiled. 'It's a funny thing because I could tell you have the moment you walked in.' My disbelief made me squeal when I asked, 'How?' Her smile didn't waver. 'It takes one to know one, I guess.' I somehow finished the rest of my question. 'Does depression still leave you feeling anxious?'

My shoulders hunched forward as Padukone spoke. 'There's always that anxiety, and this is something that I keep asking my doctors: What if this happens again?' she said. The actor then looked at me and her hand pointed in my direction. 'You've experienced it, and it has probably been the worst experience of your life.' No stranger had ever addressed my depression so directly, and I could only nod. 'If you were aware of what your symptoms were, you'd perhaps have spoken to someone about it. For me, the scariest bit was the not knowing. I didn't know what I was going through.' The interview soon started to resemble the meeting of a mental health support group. When Padukone said, 'It's hard to pull yourself out of bed, to put on a front, especially when something else is going on in your mind,' I said emphatically, 'I know exactly what you mean.' My last few questions were all trivial in comparison.

I called my sister from the foyer of the hotel. 'Deepika Padukone and I had a moment,' I said excitedly. 'In your head you have a moment with every woman you think is pretty, but more importantly, what was she wearing?' came her reply.

I was annoyed when I said, 'Denim, from head to toe. But I'm not kidding you. It really was a moment.' I could hear my niece cry in the background. 'Great! I have to go now,' said my sister. 'I'll call you soon.' All the enthusiasm that had

[handwritten margin note: Connection w feelings of depression (& dwent disorminate)]

goaded me into calling her started to dissipate. The empathy with which Padukone had recognized me as a depressive was winsome, but it was also terrifying in its accuracy. I had begun to turn down every invitation I received from adamant friends. In three months, I hadn't finished a single book I had started, and waking up in time for breakfast had become difficult. It was only my professional diligence that helped disguise my very private melancholy. Even though I was no alien to depression, Padukone had identified symptoms I had not been able to. I thought of calling my doctors, but scared I would set off an alarm and offer proof of my mood being inconsistent again, I only took one tablet of lithium that night, instead of the prescribed two. I believed I knew depression well enough to cure it. Left unfettered, the bipolar mind is naturally inclined to chase the high of mania. Though hopeless and despondent, I didn't want the madness of a manic breakdown. I just wanted to borrow some of its elation.

~

In the 1980s, middle-class families in Calcutta relied on a set of material signifiers—air conditioners, Maruti 800s, holidays in Puri—to convince themselves of an affluence that was often devised. My parents could not escape the cliché, and for much of my childhood, the beach in Puri was my horn of plenty.

I'd build sandcastles with my sister and we'd excitedly chase camels. We would stand at the edge of the sea, waiting for the waves to wet our toes. My mother, who would sit in her oversized T-shirt a few feet away, would shout maniacally if she saw the water had reached our thighs. 'I won't drown, Ma,' I told her after she had once yelled at me for walking too far in. 'More than you drowning,' she confessed, 'I'm scared of not being able to find you. I don't know how to swim, and this sea is too big.'

My mother's fear was easy to internalize, and ever since that day she had lightly spanked my bottom for my boyish imprudence, the immeasurability of the sea had scared me far more than the depths of its waters. Though the ocean is an apt and easy metaphor for eternity, I had always thought the idea was too daunting to comprehend. When faced with a force that has no beginning or end, all the significance I had so painstakingly invented for myself would then be nullified in an instant. The worry was never that the sea would kill me. I was only disquieted by the fact that it'd do so with indifference.

On 24 January 2016, when my taxi picked up speed on the Bandra–Worli Sea Link, I eased my head out of its window to let my tongue lap at the wind. Surrounded by the Arabian Sea, Bombay can be unkind to those who dread the ocean, but at two-thirty in the morning, with serotonin, dopamine, adrenaline and alcohol coursing through me, I felt indomitable. I had given up on lithium and sleep.

Amused by my manic unravelling, Mahesh, the cab driver, looked in his rear-view mirror and said, 'You seem to have had a lot of fun tonight, sir.' I was in the mood for histrionics. 'There is no sorrow in the world that four Patiala pegs of whisky can't cure.' Mahesh reached for a switch near his steering wheel, and his black-and-yellow cab was suddenly an electric neon blue. 'I put these on for all my customers who like to party,' he said with a laugh.

As he began to zip across the remaining kilometres of an almost empty bridge, the sea, as seen from Mahesh's

disco taxi, was pitch-black. If not for the light of a distant
steamer, the night would have swallowed whole the horizon
too. 'Sometimes I feel very scared of the sea,' I confessed to
Mahesh, hoping to forge a familiarity. The tone he soon
acquired was reassuring. He said, 'Think about this Sea Link,
sir. Look at the Haji Ali Dargah. These are all in the middle
of the sea. We built these. Man built these. There is nothing
we cannot conquer. The sky, the forest, the ocean—we can
go anywhere. We can even go underground, into hell. We
were born to rule this world. There is nothing to be afraid
of. And as long as you are in my car, you don't need to be
scared of anything. Mahesh is always here.' I was comforted
by Mahesh's Darwinism. His protection only amplified my
chutzpah. I told myself I was not frightened by the sea, by
eternity or by him.

Born in Allahabad, Mahesh did not seem nostalgic when
talking about his home town in Uttar Pradesh. 'I came here
when I was nine, and I have lived here for twenty years now.
I am a pukka Mumbaikar,' he told me. With a rakish smile,
he then went on to add, 'If there is something you ever need,
legal, illegal, you just need to call me. I know where to get it
all. I love this city, and this city loves me.'

Euphoric at having finally found a crafty source who
could help me navigate Bombay's notorious nadir, I asked
Mahesh, 'Do you know where I can find a dance bar?'
Mahesh's confidence didn't peter out at this point, though I
was surprised by an unanticipated demonstration of morality.
'I know of one in Andheri, but it would have closed by now.
Why would a person like you want to go to a place like that?
It's a dirty place with dirty people,' he said. I told him I was

a journalist and that I was working on a story which required me to find the few dance bars left in the city. 'I only want to speak to some of the girls who work there, nothing else.'

Mahesh's gregariousness came to be replaced by a reticence. 'I can help you meet one or two, but you will have to pay them. They don't do anything for free. Would you like to go tomorrow?' Lighting my cigarette in the neon light, I asked, 'Now, why not now?' Though my impatience had begun to annoy Mahesh, I imagined he was approximating his final fare when he parked his taxi to take out his phone. The hush of his whisper made it hard for me to hear the conversation, but his laughter, which till a few moments ago was ebullient, had now turned baleful. He was gruff when he turned to say, 'I don't want any trouble. My name better not be in the paper. I'm not mixed up in all this. I'm taking you there so you can talk or do whatever else you want. That isn't my problem. It's yours.' I thanked him profusely. His silence, however, soon grew threatening.

Journalists are, of course, often excited by the illicit. In any disregard of prohibition, there is subversion, and in subversion, there is almost always a story. Earlier that month, Mukul, an otherwise unassuming reporter, looked oddly enthusiastic at our Bombay newspaper's morning edit meet. He said he had credible proof that a number of drinking holes in the city were in fact a front for seamy dance bars the state government had banned in 2005. A senior colleague quipped, 'I think dance bars are like Schrödinger's Garfield. Even if they're alive, their dancers will all be lazy and listless.' Despite this cynicism, I agreed to help investigate and write the story. From the visuals I had seen and the stories I had heard, dance

bars had resisted transformation in the twenty-odd years
they had flourished. Change had only been incremental. The
waistband of the dancer's skirt had slipped below her belly
button by an inch or two. Her blouse showed a little more
back. Waiters still wore bow ties, and though the crooner still
wore a sequined jacket, the innuendos of his songs had all
but lost their bashfulness. The burly businessman might have
tottered some more, but the skill with which he scattered
cash remained just as artful. Sleaze, the pictures made clear,
defied time.

Staying back at work after hours, Mukul and I painted
a picture of a dance bar which had been forced to rely on
stealth for survival. 'Anything that goes underground can only
become seedier. I think we should go to one of these bars,
order a couple of beers, and the story will write itself,' Mukul
said. Like all hardened crime reporters, he was fascinated by
both plot and procedure. 'The atmosphere is important, but
I'd like to be able to ask the dancers how they felt when their
bars were outlawed,' I added. Mukul grew animated, 'There
were seventy-five thousand of them in the state, so I want to
know how they have reacted to the Supreme Court's ruling
that the 2005 ban on their workplace was unconstitutional.'
Mukul's phone book was a veritable map to Bombay's
underbelly, and we mined it for the numbers of police officials,
gangsters and bar owners. A week later, though, none of his
dependable contacts had helped us with an address. 'These
dance bars exist, but only an Indiana Jones can help you find
them,' an activist said, chuckling at my desperation. After our
colleagues grew bored of winking at us in the hallway, we too
lost our pluck, but sitting in Mahesh's cab a fortnight later,

I had started to feel hopeful again. I texted Mukul: 'Where there is a will, there's a dance bar. I've found one.'

I checked my watch to see Mahesh had been driving us through an unusually vacant Bombay for well over an hour. He had turned off his neon lights, and we had long left behind a city and sea I could recognize. My palms were sweaty. I didn't just fear being robbed. I waited for my belly to first be stabbed and then slit from right to left. My body would be left in a dump for dogs to chew and garbage collectors to haul. I was manic enough to not want to put up a fight. The violence I imagined was corporeal and, in that moment, seductive. When Mahesh pulled up outside a McDonald's in Andheri at four-thirty in the morning, the sky was still inky, but the pavement he had parked beside was fortuitously well lit. 'Take this number,' he instructed. 'Tell the man I brought you here. I've spoken to him. He'll come and pick you up. Also, you owe me two thousand rupees. That's my fare and my commission.' I didn't haggle. His manner was no longer protective, and the gore I had imagined left me in a hurry to escape. Seeing me count my change, Mahesh laughed and said, 'I think you should visit the ATM down there. You are going to need more money, at least ten thousand more.'

Mahesh did not display the geniality of an accomplice or the charity of a benefactor, and I was happy to see him drive away. I dialled the number he had given. No one answered. Still sanguine, I stepped into the nearby ATM to withdraw twenty thousand rupees. My recklessness did not seem altogether misguided. A fat wallet makes you conspicuous in dark alleys, but I had romanticized the night enough for it to seem bountiful and right. I'd deluded myself into thinking

I'd remain safe from harm. I'd have no receipt to show, so I did not expect to be reimbursed by the office, but I told myself that my discovery would be novel, that glory was always expensive, and that I would soon earn the coveted adjective 'intrepid'.

I tried the number again, but when no one picked up, I grew impatient and enraged. I tried another half a dozen times. There would be no front-page story, but worse, I would have no story to tell.

The McDonald's around the corner thankfully stayed open through the night. As I placed an order for a chicken burger and a coffee, the moment quickly lost its eroticism. I was distracted by a peppy playlist I had compiled on my iPod, and when I began to eat for the first time in twelve hours, my body delighted in sudden nourishment. It wasn't long before food reminded me of my fatigue. Sitting on the bench outside, I didn't have the strength to finish my coffee or my cigarette. I rested my head on the seated figure of Ronald McDonald. The clown's smile was more manic than mine. A light breeze had begun to make me feel snug despite where I found myself, and closing my eyes, drifting off to sleep, I was proud I had finally invented hardship for real.

At six in the morning, my phone interrupted my nap. Mahesh's contact was calling me. The voice at his end was belligerent. 'Thirteen missed calls! Who is this?' I straightened up and spoke in a tone that was even. 'Mahesh sent me.' All I needed was a suit and a suitcase to feel more like a gangster from a '70s potboiler.

'I'm Rohit. He told me you'll be coming.'

I faked anger to disguise my renewed excitement. 'That was at four. I've been waiting here on this pavement for over two hours now,' I said.

Rohit was apologetic. 'I'm very sorry. I went off to sleep. You're at the McDonald's, right? Stay where you are. A rickshaw will pick you up in fifteen minutes.' I was afraid and I wanted specifics. 'Will the auto take me to the bar?' I could hear Rohit snigger. 'Bar? What bar?' Flustered, I exclaimed, 'The dance bar! Didn't Mahesh tell you? That's why I am here.' His silence, I felt, was excruciating. 'Oh, that's closed now. But listen, you must trust me. You will find dance and a bar where you're going. Just wait for some time. Don't go anywhere.' My curiosity made me say, 'I won't.'

I formulated a quick list of questions as I splashed my face with water in the McDonald's restroom. I imagined that all visitors to Bombay's underground were first blindfolded by their escorts and were later gagged. My nightmares betrayed my fears, and their sadism also smacked of a desire I was trying hard to ignore. But while I had felt my appetite for sex intensify in recent days, I was not going to let it infect my hunger for the perfect story. Renown mattered more than pleasure. Sitting near Ronald McDonald again, I felt his glee mock my tumult. Violence seemed likely and I had no hope of rescue. I had not told Mukul where I was going, and, scared of being misunderstood, I could think of no one I could call. Only evidence would give my journalism audacity. Without it, I was just a punter with twenty thousand rupees in his pocket, desperate for his fix.

The new sun seemed to give my transgressions some sanction, however. A few minutes later, I received a call from a number I did not recognize. 'Are you wearing a blue shirt?' asked a woman's voice. I scanned the windows on the street before I replied, 'Yes, I am. Who are you though?' Being watched left me thrilled, not scared. 'An auto will stop in front of you right now. Just get into it.' I rearranged the few possessions in my bag, and with its straps dangling from my shoulders like a schoolboy, I stood expectantly on the pavement. There were already four people in the three-wheeler that stopped beside me. Hanging from the driver's seat was a lanky man in his twenties. He gestured in my direction, asking me to get in. As I went to sit in the back seat, two women squeezed themselves in, accommodating my girth and my bag. My body brushed against the woman who was sitting beside me. 'We just spoke,' she said, shaking my hand. I looked ahead. 'Oh, so you are the shy type,' she smiled.

The woman on my right was chubbier than the quiet, scrawny girl who sat in the corner, and it was she who did much of the talking. 'My name is Divya, and my friend's name is Preeti. What's your name? What are you in the mood for?' My manic mind, I found, wanted to play, but it also wanted shelter. 'I am Advaita,' I said, 'and I'm really only in the mood to talk.' Divya laughed with a sassiness I mistook to be derision. 'Only talk? Who are you, Rajesh Khanna?'

I felt disarmed. 'I just wanted to know all about the dance bar where you work.' Putting her arm around me, Divya said, 'We don't work in a bar. We work in a hotel. We only go to the bar, so we can get work in the hotel.' I was confused. 'So you're telling me that you girls don't dance?' Divya held my cheek with her right hand and said, 'Of course we do, but for that the charge is extra.' She had begun to unnerve me. This was not the story I had set out to write.

Divya straightened up to ask, 'How long would you like to talk to us for?' I told her an hour would be enough. 'That would be ten thousand rupees,' she said, 'and an extra two thousand rupees for the hotel room.' Taking out my wallet, I was counting the money when she asked, 'Which one of us would you like?' My feminism left me dumbfounded. 'No, I can't do that,' I said. 'I can't choose.' Divya soothed my head with her fingers. 'It's only human to have taste. Don't worry. Neither of us will feel bad.' Preeti, who until now had sat almost motionless, pointed her thumb to her floral shirt with a smile that was both seductive and vulnerable. 'I'll take Preeti,' I said.

The lobby of the hotel where Divya left me was the size of an office cubicle. Introducing himself from behind the reception desk, Rohit said, 'I'm so sorry I fell asleep, sir. It was a busy night. But you should know that our services are available twenty-four seven.' Annoyed that I had been led to a brothel instead of a dance bar, I snapped, 'Your friend Mahesh lied to me. This is not what I had asked for.' Rohit was not interested in my complaint. 'Let all that be, sir. I will make sure that all your needs are met. We will just need you to pay three thousand rupees and we'll need you to deposit with us some identification.' I was certain that Rohit's amiability only masked his capacity for extortion, and for a few hours now, my expenditure had stopped being my main concern. Handing him the cash, I looked for my voter ID card. No longer could I attribute my excess to Advaita Goswami. I'd have to take responsibility for my infractions.

The room I was ushered into had no windows. There would be no quick getaway. When Rohit asked if I'd need anything, I asked for coffee and an ashtray. 'Preeti will bring those with her shortly,' he said, while shutting the aluminium door behind him. The sheets looked worn but clean. Sitting cross-legged on the bed, I closed my eyes, hoping my posture would funnel the restraint of an ascetic. Unlike my judgement, my rigour had not deserted me, and if I persevered enough, I thought I might still find a story to report. I was toying with my phone when Preeti walked in with condoms, coffee and an ashtray.

Leaving them on the bedside table, she reached to unbutton her jeans. 'That won't be necessary,' I told her. 'Why don't you just sit down, so that we can talk?' She looked puzzled. 'You are a funny one,' she said suspiciously. Preeti asked if she could borrow a cigarette when I lit mine. Taking a drag, she screwed up her nose. 'What is this, menthol?' I nodded. 'You better be careful. These cigarettes, I have heard, destroy your desire.'

Preeti and I sat smoking on opposite ends of the inordinately large bed. The meekness that had defined her disposition in the rickshaw had now been replaced by a refreshing chattiness. I told her I was a journalist and that I had a few questions I wanted to put to her. 'I will not use your name. Your photo will not come out in the paper. You don't need to worry. But tell me, how old are you?' Rubbing the freckles on her cheek, she said, 'I am twenty-three.' For once, I felt little need for a typed questionnaire. 'And where are you from?' My face broke into a goofy grin the second she said 'Benares'.

For close to five minutes, we discussed Benares's street food, the lane where she lived, the traffic, the cows and the Ganga. Our exchange soon lost the formality of a transaction. Sprawling herself on the bed, lighting another of my cigarettes, Preeti told me she had come to Bombay when she was twenty-one. 'I used to first work in an office, but there was such little money there. This job is so much better.' I had started to feel priggish and oddly protective. 'But don't the men sometimes get violent?' I asked. Preeti looked at me with some contempt. 'I'm a big girl. I can look after myself.'

Preeti soon grew more talkative. If I could only dig a little deeper, I'd find a headline.

'So, tell me a little more about the bar that Divya was talking about.' Removing her short hair from her face, Preeti said, 'If we don't find ourselves a client by the evening, we go hang out at this bar nearby. The men don't always pay well, but you will always get business.' I persevered. 'And you don't dance at this bar?' She chuckled. 'Is this some kind of fetish you have? No, if we danced there, the cops would take us away in no time.' Feeling crestfallen, I chose to remain adamant. 'And is that something you're used to, run-ins with cops?' I asked. Trying to blow a smoke ring, Preeti replied, 'This hotel was raided last year. They took us away for a few days, but after that, we haven't really had any trouble.' Seeing me gulp, Preeti got up to uncross my legs. She spread them wide and turned to rest her back on my chest. Running her fingers through mine, she asked, 'Do you really not want to do anything?' I nestled my chin in the nape of her neck. 'I really don't,' I assured her. 'Do you have some kind of problem?' she asked. I couldn't help but laugh. 'I do have many problems, yes, but I only came here to work, nothing else.'

In the next ten minutes, Preeti told me that having recently discovered gin, she had grown to hate beer. She didn't like going to the movies—'they are so unreal'—and her father, she said, was a pious man, who, however, feared his daughters more than God. 'Will you come with me to a Shiva temple tomorrow?' The nonchalance with which Preeti had asked me this question made it seem altogether trivial. There was something moving about the familiarity of her request, something auspicious in her mention of Shiva, but rather than significance, I found myself wrought with guilt. The friendship I was trying to fashion had little sincerity, and for the first time that day, I asked myself the question, 'What am I doing here?'

In what seemed like an instant, I finally became aware of my imprudence and its possible consequence. 'I think it's time I left,' I said, gently moving Preeti forward. Confused by my capriciousness, she earnestly implored, 'Don't leave. You still have a lot of time left.' Picking up my bag, I said, 'I have to go.' Seeing me unlock the door, she asked, 'Can you give me two thousand rupees? I have these bills to pay.' Desperate and panicky, I emptied my wallet on the bed. 'I'll call you,' she cried.

In the course of five hours, I had spent a third of my savings. I had risked arrest and harm. Worse still, I had not found a story that could justify my abandon. Rather than regret, though, I felt the exhilaration of the newly free. I again stuck my head out of the cab I had found, elated to feel the sun on my face. Ten minutes later, I felt my heart sink. I realized Rohit still had my voter ID. Having made my way back to the hotel, I received a text from Preeti. 'I'm bored,' she'd typed. Standing at the reception, waiting for Rohit to find my card, I replied, 'I think you should get some sleep. I'm so sorry if I kept you up.'

The next morning, I felt heroic. I had escaped Bombay's underground, and had brought with me notes I wanted to share with my colleagues. I told Mukul, 'I spent half my salary in that brothel last night, but it was worth it. I have a story!' He looked incredulous. A senior editor asked, 'So, did you have to shower all your cash in that dance bar?' I smiled. 'I didn't make it there, but the place I found was bigger, better.' Abha, a member of my team, looked stricken. 'Is it true?' she asked. 'You spent last night with a prostitute?' I snapped. 'She has a name—Preeti; and yes, I spent last night with her. She was a delight.'

It didn't take long for the euphoria to get the better of me. I put in my papers before I could file a story I had widely advertised as the 'biggest scoop of my career', and when Preeti called to ask for eleven thousand rupees in February, I said, 'I don't have a job. I don't have any money. If you ask me, you should quit too. It is a world of fun.' I never did hear from her after that day.

~

When reduced to a sum of their symptoms, bipolar patients are often indistinguishable. Stories of mania and depression only have to be slightly tweaked for them to be relatable. Watching the first season of *Homeland* in 2011, I sat with a checklist. Carrie Mathison, the bipolar protagonist of the American television series, immediately seemed like a counterpart. Her moods, like mine, were erratic. You needed subtitles when she began speaking at breakneck speed. Mania made her promiscuous too, and like me, she spent much of her time piecing together impossible jigsaws. I'd feel like a saviour when I'd draw parallels between Dostoevsky and the Koran, but for Carrie, saving the world was a real mandate. As a CIA agent, she was tasked with an almost messianic responsibility. She had to ensure that the horrors of 9/11 did not repeat themselves. Giving a headline, for me, was sometimes a matter of life and death. For Carrie, however, that distinction was literal. She made a scene, yes, but she got the job done.

Though bipolarity gives *Homeland* some of its many thrills, the series, in effect, tells the rare story of a manic-depressive at the workplace. Initially, Carrie hides her condition from her bosses and colleagues. The CIA, she is perhaps wise in assuming, would not be too comfortable putting the security of its country's citizens in the hands of someone certifiably 'crazy'.

When diagnosed in 2007, my psychiatrist had advised I disguise my first episode of mania as a bout of cerebral malaria. 'You might find that your colleagues don't take too kindly to the idea that you suffer from a mental illness that is persistent,' he had said. It didn't, however, take long for my bipolarity to become common knowledge, and I thought it only prudent to disclose details of my affliction each time I was interviewed for a new position. The support Carrie eventually finds at the CIA is fortunately abundant in the offices of the Indian media. I invariably found myself struck by the compassion of my editors. My candour, they said, was refreshing, but their empathy did come with a caveat. 'Don't tell HR about this and please don't give up on those medicines.'

Without ever bringing out the kid gloves, my employers quietly reined in my penchant for detecting patterns the few times I got carried away. I was never castigated when my depression made me slow or when my mania made me incoherent. I was treated equally and often given a free hand. Much like Carrie, my work consumed me, and in moments when words and ideas were wilful, I too idealized a past when my mind had not been encumbered by the clogs of lithium. Carrie once tells her lover, 'The meds have saved my life, literally, but something is lost too. There's this window, when you've got all this crazy energy, but you're still lucid, you're still making sense and that's always when I did my best work.' Mental health practitioners have given Carrie's 'window' a more officious name—hypomania, a term they use to describe the early phases of mania. Hypomania brings with it a euphoria that is untouched by aggression, a percipience that is not yet tinged with belligerence. To chase that sweet spot of wondrous clarity, to make it perpetual, Carrie throws her prescription out the window.

Her lead has been easy to follow. But while hypomania makes my mind dexterous and my writing nimble, it also makes me forget that mania is precipitous. Carrie pays a price for her defiance. She is institutionalized. Predictably, I was too.

Much to the amusement of my colleagues, I began colour-coding my notes and books a few years after I was diagnosed. The shaded classification helped give my journalism and reading an order my mind was sometimes resolved to disrupt. To mark something vital, I used my purple pen. If I came across prose I envied, I brought out my pink highlighter. Black was used in the margins of books, and green always meant 'rework'. When Saul Berenson, Carrie's boss and mentor, first comes to visit her in the hospital, he only wants to check on her bruises. Worryingly, he finds her bringing her ward down with the unreasonable yet urgent demand for a green pen. He thankfully has one on him. Though her speech is hurried and her thoughts are muddled, it's the green pen that gives Carrie away. Saul soon realizes his protégé is bipolar.

The relationship that a mercurial Carrie shares with the more sober Saul sustains her and much of *Homeland*. Saul, the CIA's Middle East division chief, does not feel disillusioned when he is made aware of Carrie's manic depression. He demonstrates remorse instead. He should have read the signs better. He feels sorry for not having asked her if she was all right. Spending his nights watching over her, he edits her work and breaks down her codes of colour. Saul does not lose faith in Carrie. He delights in her genius. When a repentant Carrie signs up for electroconvulsive therapy, he storms into her hospital, pulls the drip from her hand and warns her against a treatment he thinks is unnecessary and dramatic. Eventually, he makes it possible for her to return to the CIA. Saul's solicitude enables Carrie's trust, but her want for his approval far exceeds her desire for forbearance. His paternal warmth is easy to idealize. It guarantees survival, but more importantly, it facilitates fulfilment.

Almost every time I am manic, I seek out my first editor, a man I have fondly called 'Boss' since 2005. Having once likened him to *Mad Men*'s Don Draper, I declared to him in 2013, 'You're my Saul.' I felt my second comparison was watertight. An iconoclast who prized authenticity over sycophancy, my attentive mentor met me at a time when my sudden moments of inspiration and proficiency had not yet been delineated by a diagnosis. He parachuted me into Kabul and Beirut when I was working with a national paper, edited my clumsy copy and taught me the fundamentals of a journalism that is accountable.

In 2007, two months after I had impulsively quit my job, I began calling him at all hours of the day and night. 'Boss, there's a thread that ties everything,' I once announced excitedly, and rather than respond with exasperation, he was indulgent. My editor came to see me in a Delhi hospital in 2010. My mouth dripped with drool and my fingers shook uncontrollably. I was ashamed. I had never wanted him to see me at my worst. He, however, joked that my manic episodes were like 'meteor showers'. A few months later, he offered me the position of foreign editor at a newspaper he helmed and gave me a cubicle in his Bombay office.

A year into the job, I'd keep inventing excuses to leave, and when I went to resign for the second time in eight months, his rage matched Saul's. 'You're the smartest and dumbest fucking person I've ever known,' Saul once tells Carrie. 'A world exists outside that damn head of yours. Be more responsible if you want to live in it,' I was told sharply. There were occasions when my caprice exhausted his patience, but his kindness never flinched.

Psychiatrists often use the word 'trigger' when listing the causes that precipitate an attack of mania, unwittingly likening them to firearms just waiting to go off. Manic-depressives are warned to steer clear of stress, the most pernicious and inevitable of all triggers. Carrie chases terrorists and deconstructs their malignant game plans. Few jobs in the world are quite as stressful as hers. For me, regrettably, editing restaurant reviews was sometimes calamitous enough. Deadlines would come to seem oppressive and words would be impossible to order.

Working for a national magazine in Delhi, I walked into the office one day, gregarious, no longer my conscientious self. I kept leaving my desk to smoke countless cigarettes and to have conversations that were in equal parts animated and meaningful. I declared a lasting affection for colleagues I barely knew, and while listing luxury items, I haughtily quoted Truman Capote. It didn't take long for two of my senior editors to see I was manic. 'Why don't you take the day off, Shreevatsa?' one of them said. 'We've bought you a ticket to Calcutta. Go home for the weekend. Meet your family. You're in such a good mood. They'd like to see you.' Being driven to the airport, I said, 'I don't want to be removed from society.' My beneficent senior smiled. 'Look at this as preservation instead.' Three days later, I sat in my analyst's chair and said, 'My editors in Delhi are the parents I've always wanted.'

In 2005, a sympathetic assistant editor in her mid-thirties rescued me from the cliché of being a coffee-ferrying intern by giving me my first journalistic assignment. Her quasi-maternal affection and generosity led to a bunch of us fledgling reporters calling her 'Ma'. I took this joke very seriously. Free of the ferment, baggage and responsibility that define the relationships children share with their parents, I found in the rituals of my flippant adoption a plenitude I felt I had all but lost. My adopted mother sometimes cooked me lunch, gave me relationship advice and took pride in my ordinary professional successes. There was a joy in the obfuscation of the personal and the professional, and so when I was manic years later, inconsolable, crying in front of another, much older department head, I told her, 'You remind me of my grandmother.' She said, 'But that's not someone I ever wanted to be.'

Defeated and despondent, I texted a colleague later that day, 'You should've said there's no Saul. There never was.'

~

When mania begins to keep you up at night, forcing you to lose inhibition, no detail seems trivial. Only you know the import of a story because only you can read between the lines. Carrie Mathison, a hardened intelligence officer, uses these penetrative insights to foil multiple terror plots, but as a journalist, I found my judgement suffered because of the excitability of my new intuitiveness. Devouring the news, I saw a headline even in the most innocuous of events. In 2016, having led a team of five writers for six months, I started readily approving ideas I'd otherwise dismiss as hare-brained and half-baked. Nothing was impossible and I had lost the ability to say no.

With the year's Academy Awards around the corner, I was intent on savouring one Best Picture nominee after another. Though my 2016 work planner was already looking crammed, I took on the responsibility of reviewing these films for my Bombay newspaper. Quentin Tarantino's bloody and macabre *The Hateful Eight*, I felt, could be explained by the image of the crucifix which opens the film—'Man, a victim of his inherent nature, will sin.' *Spotlight*, I told everyone I met, was 'the most important movie ever made'. The film, which told the story of four journalists investigating charges of child abuse against the Boston clergy, was one I effortlessly identified with. I was not just finding myself in the stories cinema had to tell. I *was* the story.

I was awake when the day's papers were left on my doorstep on the morning of 18 January. Not yet an eight-column headline, I found buried in a corner of the front page a little item that detailed the discovery of a student's body in Hyderabad. Rohith Vemula, a twenty-five-year-old PhD scholar, had used the room of a friend to hang himself. The report made mention of his caste—he was a Dalit—but was otherwise stingy with details. The correspondent did not, for instance, elaborate on the chain of events which had led to Rohith's suicide.

There is something obviously electric about seeing a news story gain momentum. In just a few hours, the Internet began to fill the blanks the national dailies had left. Rohith's history was arguably typical. Having defied the limits of his persecuted caste with scholarships, he then found in student politics a stage where he could perform his identity, a megaphone that would compensate for his lack of a voice. He protested the hanging of a convicted terrorist, he idolized Che Guevara and fought hard against the hegemony of right-wing activists. His revolt soon became conspicuous. The university stopped paying him his stipend. The Narendra Modi–led central government took seriously accusations that his activities were 'casteist' and 'anti-national'. Removed from his college hostel, he was later suspended.

The empathy I soon came to feel was hysterical and wholehearted. Rohith's circumstances helped put me in his shoes, but it was his suicide letter, lucid and proud, that helped me tie my laces the way he would. Calling himself a 'monster', the scholar wrote, 'I feel a growing gap between my soul and my body.' My obsession with the note only doubled when I read, 'I always wanted to be a writer.' People, he said, had divorced themselves from nature. 'Our feelings are second handed. Our love is constructed. Our beliefs coloured. Our originality valid through artificial art. It has become truly difficult to love without getting hurt.' His pathos had punch. I thought I could even detect a sly, dark humour. 'I am writing this kind of letter for the first time. My first time of a final letter,' he had written. Disregarding the relevance of caste, I thought he was articulating my private anguish when he wrote, 'My birth is my fatal accident. I can never recover from my childhood loneliness.' Rohith had offered his oppressors adequate absolution—'Do not trouble my friends and enemies on this after I am gone'—and he had also demonstrated in his letter a resignation I desperately wanted to emulate. 'I am not sad,' he admitted, 'I am just empty. Unconcerned about myself. That's pathetic. And that's why I am doing this.'

I had memorized Rohith's suicide note. Marching into my editor's office, I exclaimed to her, 'I could've written that letter.' There was something unseemly about my sudden lack of restraint. All the texts I had ever sent her began with an apology. I was atoning for the imposition of my messages, yes, but also secretly for the sluggishness of my depression. Every email I sent ended with a note of gratitude. I could never thank her enough.

If I needed to see her, I would purposefully loiter outside her room, waiting to be noticed. That Tuesday, however, I was boisterous. Seeing me barge in with a printout of Rohith Vemula's last words, my editor only looked up from her desktop and smiled. 'You could've written that letter, but I am glad you didn't.' I was speaking faster than usual. 'This really could bring the BJP government down.' I had her attention. 'And how will that happen?' she asked. 'All the Opposition needs to do is go from one village to another and tell the country's Dalit populace, "The prime minister killed Rohith Vemula." Given the facts, they wouldn't be all wrong.' My editor looked perturbed. She asked me to sit down. 'It's not always like that, Shreevatsa.'

I crossed my legs and tapped the floor restlessly with my right foot. 'A suicide can be political, of course it can, but I think you're forgetting that it is psychological first,' she said. I wasn't in the mood to back down and I countered, 'But here we are talking about a mind that had been bruised by caste discrimination since its very inception. Surely psychology can't help but include politics.' My conviction, I thought, was contagious. 'So, what do you do you want to do about this?' she asked. 'I think our package next Sunday should be comprehensive. Two in-depth stories, one reported from Hyderabad and the other from Bombay. The first story will detail the immediate impact of Rohith's suicide, and the second will look at the prevalent caste bias which plagues our city's colleges and universities.' My editor's frown betrayed her consternation. 'That's a sweeping statement. You have no proof of that.' I remained adamant. 'I'll get a reporter to find you proof. For a Dalit who still has to suffer the tag of untouchability, I fear, prejudice will always be palpable.' Though unconvinced, she relented. 'I'll know it when I see it. I'd like to see the stories once they're in. Also, are you all right?' I beamed. 'Never better!'

It doesn't always take long for hypomanic energy and confidence to transform into manic disruption and arrogance. Over the course of just four days, I found myself enraged by the apathy of institutions that had forced Rohith Vemula to hang from the ceiling of a room that was not his. My initial investment in the story had now metamorphosed into a greater fury. I was snapping at my colleagues. I was short with my teammates, and my frequent Facebook posts were slowly turning truculent. The diligence with which I edited the dispatch from Hyderabad was unusual. I relied on more than three sources when cross-checking the reporter's facts. I had seen pictures of the room where Rohith grew up. I knew he hated spending his days in a laboratory. I thought I knew how he would think. I'd grown obsessed with the justice he'd found elusive.

On 23 January, I saw in my inbox the evidence my editor had sought. The education correspondent of our Bombay newspaper had found that discrimination in the city's colleges and universities was not just implicit, it was tangible.

A Dalit student was reduced to a servant by her research guide. She had only contemplated suicide, but a more disconsolate peer had hurled himself down from the sixth

floor of a building. Rohith Vemula was only a symptom.
Bigotry was a more ubiquitous pandemic. That Saturday, I
walked into the office with some purpose. I went up to our
illustrator and said, 'I have a story that hits the nail on the
head, it is the last nail in the coffin of the system. Do you
know Martin Luther? Do you remember the letter he nailed
on the door of the church? Let's draw a gate. We'll create an
arch. We'll write "Mumbai's House of Learning" on it and
we'll pin to the wood Rohith Vemula's suicide note.' I could
see he was carried away by my ardour.

My editor, however, was more circumspect. 'The story
is hardly objective. It never gives the other side a chance to
defend itself,' she said. I retorted, 'If I had to choose between
objectivity and truth, I'd choose the latter.' Her tone didn't
waver. 'But forsaking objectivity will only make you an
activist, not a journalist.'

That evening, my editor vetted my every decision. The
illustration I had suggested was disregarded. My immoderate
headlines were tweaked, and my pages were sent to press
twenty minutes past their usual deadline. My sulk lasted the
weekend. I was called to my editor's room on Monday.

'Things got a little out of hand on Saturday,' she told me,
asking me to sit down. I clicked my pen and said, 'I just felt the
Rohith Vemula story struck at the heart of all that was wrong
with this country.' She looked solicitous. 'I know this story
affected you deeply, but you know an attachment so deep can
be detrimental, right?' I sounded aggrieved when I countered,
'Isn't a passionate journalist better than an indifferent one?'

My response surprised her. She said, 'You need to tell
me what is wrong. Something seems to have shifted.' The

concern in her voice softened me. 'I know that some people will call this mania, but this time it's different. It is a shift in consciousness,' I said. My editor did not let her incredulity show. 'What do your doctors say?' she asked. 'They do believe such a shift is possible.' That commitment I had to truth was proving precarious. 'And is this shift new? Have you ever felt it happen before?' I looked her in the eye. 'I do think it has, but I was never quite able to control it.'

Before leaving, I turned to her and said, 'I made headway with that bar dancer story yesterday.' After I had described to her my early-morning cab ride with Mahesh, told her about the twenty thousand rupees I'd spent, and had shown her Preeti's texts, she said, 'You don't have a story yet.' I was upbeat, saying, again, 'Where there's a will, there's a dance bar!' She prescribed caution. 'Be careful out there.'

Over the next week, I found that I had all but forgotten the geniality of our conversation. Mania, I found, had a strange habit of arriving when I had money in the bank account to exhaust. As I went through my savings, I would also give up my desire for accumulation. My madness made me a big spender, yes, but it made me a renunciant too. I abjured materialism even as I spent more money in the shops I impulsively walked into.

I did not want to be co-opted by the very economy and system that had forced Rohith Vemula to take his life. On a flight to Calcutta, I convinced myself that the mainstream media which paid me a salary was also guilty of perpetuating an evil that made Rohith's and my good untenable. Minutes after landing, I called my editor and told her, 'I'd like to quit and I'm afraid my ethics will not allow me to serve a notice period.'

She didn't sound irate or disappointed. 'That's fine. Don't worry about it, but are you all right?' I replied, 'No, but I'll get there soon. Also, I wanted to thank you. Something you said gave me the title for a book. "It's not always like that." It really isn't.'

8

Coming Up for Air

In his slim but seminal book *Strictly Bipolar*, British psychoanalyst and author Darian Leader writes that in the memoirs of many manic-depressive subjects, 'pages of disappointment with mental health workers and medication will almost invariably be followed by a sentence such as: "Then I met the best doctor."' More than the greatest doctor or the perfect drug, Leader suggests, what helps a bipolar subject is 'the actual function of idealization itself'. By idealizing our doctors and therapists, we safeguard their authority and make them parental substitutes, someone who embodies a 'consistent and benevolent gaze'.

Resisting the temptation of such glorification has been impossible for me, but Dr Pushpa Misra and Dr C.S. Mukherji have both received punctured declarations of my immeasurable debt. 'It's because of you that I get my second chances, doctor,' I once told Dr Misra. 'You pick yourself up, Shreevatsa,' she said, 'but the trouble is that your slippers are quite slippery.'

The efficacy of doctors is often measured by the frequency with which their patients fall ill. Manic-depressives often

179

make that barometer unreliable. Notoriously non-compliant, they refuse their medicines when they are tired of their side effects, and frustrated by its slow and incremental benefits, they reject therapy. I once told Dr Mukherji, 'I think you like having me depressed. Isn't it possible for me to be manic and control its damage too? I miss feeling alive.'

A week later, I had written myself a tapered prescription, and even though I had begun to feel the effusion of hypomania, I kept my transgression secret. Tired of living in Calcutta, knocking its lack of professional and recreational opportunities, I interrupted Dr Misra's therapy and moved cities in 2013. Once away, I again turned to marijuana to cope with the stresses of employment and the paresis of depression. Predictably, mania did not take long to arrive.

Finding me unwilling to return, my doctors have had to acquiesce to my institutionalization. 'Confinement is something I don't believe in,' Dr Mukherji told me, 'but your shenanigans sometimes leave me with little choice.'

~

In July 2007, when I woke up with my hands tied to a hospital bed, I had no memory of having been brought there. My glasses had been taken off. Though everything in the room was a blur, the tiles, I saw, were a dirty green, and the tube light, I remember, flickered dolefully. I thought my male nurse's white shirt and trousers were part of his police uniform. 'Have I been arrested?' I asked him. My guilt precipitated my fear.

For six weeks, my actions had grown increasingly perilous and I was altogether indifferent to their consequence.

Accusing my parents of neglect, I had left home in a huff. I had openly berated the state and its control. I had sidled up to an Australian woman in a bikini. There was something obviously blasphemous about my presumed possession of divinity. I had pretended to be Advaita Goswami, and worse, I'd littered the streets of Delhi with pages I had torn from Virginia Woolf's diary. It was hard for me to tally my transgressions or measure their effect.

I again asked the taciturn nurse, 'Am I in jail?' Preparing a syringe, he finally replied, 'You're in a hospital. The doctor will be here to see you tomorrow.' Minutes after he had jabbed my arm, my eyes grew heavy. The oblivion was welcome. I needed to escape my new reality.

The room was dark when I surfaced. I didn't know what time it was. My watch had been removed with my restraints. Removing my blanket, I desperately searched for my phone.

'It's the first thing they take away.' The nurse's voice was a whisper.

'Please, you must have a phone,' I implored him. 'I must have the right to make at least one phone call. I really need to call my sister.'

Tucking me back in, Madhu said, 'You're not meant to have any contact with the outside world, but you're safe.'

I resisted the quilt and the warmth of his consolation. 'You must understand that the doctors here have made a mistake of some sort. I'm not meant to be here. My girlfriend is waiting for me in England. We're going to get married soon. My master's course starts in a few weeks. I need to be there, not here.'

Madhu returned to his chair. 'I'm in a long-distance relationship myself,' he soon confessed. He had met his fiancée in a nursing college, and the decision to leave Kerala for Bombay, he shyly admitted, had been the hardest one he'd ever made. 'Our phones keep us alive,' he said.

Over the next hour, as we talked about his orthodox parents, the punishing cost of living in Bombay and the many hardships of love, I felt I had disarmed Madhu with my empathy. 'I'm only asking that you give me your phone for a minute,' I cajoled him. 'My sister needs to know I am here. She really must be very worried about me.'

Tentatively, Madhu reached inside his pocket and said, 'Only one call and then I'm taking this back.'

I thanked him profusely and dialled my sister's number. I discovered a fantastic solace in her 'hello'. 'You won't believe where Mum and Dad have left me. They're treating me like a prisoner here. You have to get me out. Please.'

I could hear my sister panic. Sitting in the clinic of a psychiatrist who had ordered I be admitted to a Colaba hospital, she was filling out a bipolar questionnaire at the exact moment I called her. The checklist asked her if her thoughts raced 'no more than usual', 'somewhat more than usual' or 'much more than usual'. She was asked how often she broke into song, and if she had 'quite mystical experiences'. Already distressed by the news that I was bipolar, my sister's anxiety doubled when she heard the affliction was genetic. She could, it'd follow, be bipolar too. 'I know where you are, Shivvy. You needn't worry about anything. It'll all be all right,' she said, hanging up abruptly. Rescue, I felt sure, was on its way.

The next morning, Madhu had been replaced by an orderly. He accompanied me to the washroom, and when I stood up to go for a walk, he quickly locked the door of my room. My

hospital

mind, which until only a few days earlier, was a flood of thought and colour, had now turned lumbering and bleak. Lying in bed, I tried to make sense of my confinement. I was being administered medicines around the clock. I was apparently ill, but strangely, this hospital had no visiting hours. No worried family and friends had flocked to my side. I knew I hadn't been quarantined, and I soon grew certain I was being punished.

Later that day, a portly and bespectacled doctor entered my room and introduced himself as my psychiatrist. 'What's wrong with me?' I asked Dr Aakash Joshi, sitting up, hopeful, alert. 'You are bipolar,' he said, 'but that's good news because you'll win a Nobel Prize.'

Smoothing his silver hair with his fingers, pulling up a chair, Dr Joshi rattled off a list of names, as if reading from a roll of honour. 'Vincent van Gogh, Winston Churchill, Emily Dickinson, Sylvia Plath, Leo Tolstoy, Ernest Hemingway, Virginia Woolf—they were all bipolar, all manic-depressives.'

Rolling the words 'bipolar', 'manic' and 'depressive' in my mind, I did not have the foresight to ask the doctor questions that would later come to confound me. 'For every bipolar genius, aren't there hundreds more who suffer a crippling paralysis? Didn't Virginia Woolf and Vincent van Gogh prosper only because they had never been diagnosed, because they had never been medicated? Doesn't the mind need a modicum of turbulence to thrive?'

In that moment, though, my concerns were more fundamental. 'What does "bipolar" mean?' I asked.

'It means you have a chemical imbalance in your brain, and this imbalance causes your moods to swing wildly from time to time. But there are a number of medicines that can

manage this mood disorder. You're already on some of them.'
Dr Joshi had already started checking his watch.

'But these medicines make me so groggy. I want to sleep all the time,' I complained.

'You've been up for a very long time. It is time you got some rest.'

Dr Joshi had little patience for my silence. Seeing him stand to leave, I said with some desperation, 'I know I have alienated my parents, but I would really like to see them now.'

The psychiatrist held my hand in his. 'They're not going anywhere. Let's get you all right first, and then there will be plenty of time for you to see them.'

I held on tightly to his palm. 'And when will I be fine, doctor? When will I be cured?'

There was hardly any comfort in Dr Joshi's smile. 'Bipolarity is not a disease, it is a condition. We can't cure it, but you can manage it. You'll have a normal life. I can promise you that.'

I was disconsolate. 'When will I get out of here?'

Dr Joshi removed his hand from my clutch. 'It's only been a day. You have to learn to be more patient. I'll be back tomorrow.'

I had one last question to ask. 'Where's Madhu?'

Dr Joshi frowned. 'He doesn't work here any more.'

I lay pinned to my mattress for the next forty-eight hours, and as I continued staring at the cracks in the ceiling, my back began to hurt as much as my head. Though Dr Joshi had not employed the word, it didn't take long for me to think of myself as 'mad'. My madness, however, I consoled myself, defied stereotype. I had never spoken to myself. I'd only called friends in the middle of the night, hoping someone would listen. In the six weeks of my 'mania', I had never once been violent. I'd only wanted to be the life of the party, and it was this extraversion, extravagant and exceptional, which had made the bluster of my mind conspicuous. My crime was not my grandiosity. My error was I'd foolishly let my swagger show.

Having taken over from Madhu, the chubby Sister Rita soon brought to my room an affection that was decidedly maternal. She settled my pillows every few minutes, and insisted that I drink water—'With the number of medicines you're taking, you need plenty of liquids to flush them out.' The few times I woke up in a sweat, I found her holding my hand. 'It was just a bad dream. It happens,' she would say. Caressing her rosary, she would sit in her corner and pray for me. 'I'm making sure that you have Mother Mary's blessings. I want you to have her protection.'

The Colaba hospital, I realized, was a popular destination for medical tourists from the Middle East. Taking me for little walks, Rita would leave me sitting by a window, a few inches away from burqa-clad Saudi women. When one of them glowered at my boxer shorts, Rita snapped, 'He's my son. He'll wear what he likes.'

Rita began to make sure that the television in my room was left on almost throughout the day. 'If you just lie there, you'll think of all the things you shouldn't,' she said.

Perhaps in an effort to limit the sources of my stimulation, hospital authorities had given me access to just three channels. I grew bored of Discovery documentaries. Hindi news programmes proved too shrill, and I had quickly memorized the lyrics of the few songs a music network played on loop. On one of his few visits, Dr Joshi said he had devised a solution for my weariness. 'You like foreign movies, right? You're in luck. I have a little pack of these DVDs at home. We'll get a player installed in your room tonight.'

I was ecstatic. In less than a day, I had devoured Wong Kar-wai's *Happy Together*, the 2002 Turkish film *Uzak* and Fellini's *8 ½*.

The next day, Dr Joshi came to me see me a little after ten at night. 'I have a lot of time on my hands,' he said. Together, we reviewed the films I had been watching. 'You seem to be doing much better,' he said, with a smile.

'It's nice to have done something normal after so long,' I said, relishing the buoyancy I had come to suddenly feel. 'But I'm not normal, right?'

I had become familiar with Dr Joshi's frown. 'That's precisely the mindset we want you to avoid. Besides, normal is such a subjective word. My normal would be very different from yours.'

Still recovering from the humiliation of my cuffs, I retorted, 'Being strapped to this bed certainly wasn't normal for me.'

The doctor countered my annoyance with calm. 'That was for your own safety. You do know why you were brought here, don't you?' he asked.

'All I know is that for some time, I felt this boundless confidence and energy. When did they become negative things?'

Dr Joshi, I could see, was carefully measuring my agitation with his gaze. 'They're not,' he said, 'but confidence and energy aren't the only things that you felt. From what I hear, you also felt a lot of anger.'

For the first time, I felt I was making sense of my recent tumult. 'I don't know how it happened, but suddenly I began to perceive all forms of injustice in the world. And then I understood that the world had been very unfair to me. Was it fair that I'd been abused continuously for four years as a child? I admit I felt some of that humiliation belatedly, but doesn't my cousin Satyah deserve a comeuppance?'

Though I was aware my self-pity sounded pathetic, I didn't feel the need to disguise my grief. 'Is that why you left home?' asked the psychiatrist.

'I left home because I had stupidly started blaming my parents for the violence I suffered. They didn't know better. Had they known, had I told them, I probably wouldn't be here.'

Settling his glasses, Dr Joshi continued, 'Satyah has been diagnosed with depression himself. He is on medication too. Did you know that?' I bit my lip and said, 'No, I didn't know that.' The doctor wanted to know how I felt after hearing this news. The words that came to mind were 'comeuppance', 'remorse' and 'shame', but in that moment I could only say, '"pensive" is the word I am looking for.'

Standing by my bedside, Dr Joshi said, 'Your life is going to change a little after this.' The remark left me curious. 'I do know that, but in what way?' I asked.

'For one, you'll have to be a lot more disciplined. You'll need to take your medicines when you're meant to, and you're going to have to sleep for at least eight hours every day.'

Hopeful that I'd be released, I smiled. 'That sounds doable. I think I can do that.' Patting my hand, Dr Joshi added, 'The aim is to get you back on your feet, to come to a point when all that happened does not matter any more.'

Tired of my new sluggishness, I asked the surprisingly forthcoming doctor, 'But these medicines, how long will I have to take them for?'

He said, 'We'll have to wait and watch, wait till we find the right balance. They'll reduce with time, but for now, just take what is given to you.'

'I promise I'll be patient. Pun intended,' I told him.

He laughed. 'Let's put that wordplay to good use.'

Over the next week, watching the films Dr Joshi kindly continued to supply, I was distracted from my paralysing solitude. I missed the Internet, but most of all, I missed the unaffectedness with which I had once loved Lucia. My mania had already made me break the vows of fidelity, but my depression made me a renegade. It made affection and nostalgia impossible. Finding it hard to add to the conversations Sister Rita initiated with some cheer, I returned to finding shapes in the cracks on my room's ceiling.

I had just begun to feel abjured when I saw my mother walking down the sunlit corridor of the hospital, holding a bunch of lilies in one hand and a chocolate cake in another. My tearful and overwhelming reunion with my parents would soon become a template for several more such occasions when they would unexpectedly arrive in mental health institutions to facilitate my return to society.

Their hugs were long, familiar and forgiving. My mother asked, 'Are you all right? Why have you not been eating?' I was too choked to reply. My father's query was more urgent: 'Have you been sleeping?'

I tensed up and said, 'That's all I have been doing since I got here.'

Having heard my mother deliver her brief bulletin of our family's news, I finally mustered the courage to ask, 'How was I brought here?' My friends, my father told me, had gotten me to swallow a sleeping pill. There was a van waiting outside. Four orderlies had straitjacketed me and strapped me to a stretcher, bringing me to Colaba in the dead of night.

'It was brutal to watch,' my mother confessed.

'How did you know I was bipolar?' I asked.

'We didn't, but I believe you gave yourself away with the first question you asked the doctor you were taken to meet. Not everyone starts a conversation by saying, "So, what's it going to be today? Freud? Lacan? Jung?"'

Before leaving, my father turned to me and said, 'Lucia wants to fly down from Britain to be with you. Would you like her to come?'

I answered with a categorical 'no', and then looked at my mother to ask, 'When will I get out of here?'

Giving me a kiss on my cheek, she whispered in my ear, 'Forty-eight hours.'

The day I was released, Sister Rita gave me a little Mother Mary pendant she wanted me to keep on my person at all times. 'She will keep you out of trouble,' said Rita, squeezing my hand.

Though the reception I received at my sister's house was warm, I found it hard to shake off my awkwardness. Her unease was palpable when I asked if I could borrow a razor. I needed to shave my stubble and the hair that had defiantly grown on my ears.

As I stared into the mirror, my nerves and lithium both made my fingers tremble uncontrollably. The cut on my left ear was more a gash than a nick. I stood in my sister's living room, blood dripping from my face to the floor. The look of horror on her face has been hard to forget. She grabbed the cotton. 'What've you done to yourself again?'

~

Every month, my parents would make the trip from Calcutta, and flanked by them in a hired car, I'd visit Dr Joshi's South Bombay chamber for what my family would nervously call my 'regular check-up'. The waiting room was usually packed. Three empty chairs were almost always impossible to find. The haphazardly stacked film magazines I'd flip through were all typically dated. Some of them were three to four years old. Much like my mind, Bollywood's ageing actors were all fixed in a time that had passed, in moments when they were still beautiful, still vital.

Like me, most patients were also accompanied by their families—fawning mothers, solicitous siblings and aloof fathers. My counterparts gave themselves away easily. Their legs were restless, their gaze vacant and their laughter was sudden and hysterical. One would have to wait for approximately two hours to see Dr Joshi, and in this time, clichés were only exaggerated. Dr Joshi's assistants were young and female. When they'd call a name, the gasp of us other patients was despondent, but also secretly lascivious.

As expected, Dr Joshi would have only five minutes to spare when my parents and I finally entered his room. He would scan the results of my blood tests, crack a customary joke that would invariably make my father burst into laughter, and then he'd ask how I was feeling. 'I do feel quite low sometimes, doctor,' I'd usually say. 'Hold out your hands,' he'd instruct at that point. Seeing them tremble, he'd ask, 'How many cigarettes are you smoking in a day?' I'd lie and say, 'Just six.' He would nod disapprovingly. 'Let's make that three.'

Nicotine, not lithium, I was being led to believe, had made me drop four cups of coffee and just as many plates of food. As Dr Joshi wrote me a prescription that was equally calligraphic and inscrutable, I had little time to explain my embarrassment or despair. I soon began to miss our banter in the Colaba hospital. My psychiatrist was no longer interested in the films I watched. He had little time for my stray musings.

When I told him I thought I needed conversation to make sense of my condition, he said, 'I'm going to send you to Dr Aarti Sood. She is an excellent and very patient therapist. She is just the person you need to see.' I felt like a parcel he'd just passed on.

Dr Sood's therapist's chamber seemed too small for the number of New Age totems that crammed its every cranny. I was easily distracted by her feng shui crystals, Buddhist wall hangings and butter lamps, but it was really her diamonds and pearls that ambushed my concentration. Her manner was that of a socialite and I found her advice correspondingly incredible.

'You know Zaheer Khan, the cricketer?' she once asked me. 'It's hard not to know him,' I said. 'I was watching him on TV the other day,' she went on, 'and he really reminded me of you.' I giggled and said, 'But I don't have a single athletic bone in my body, doctor, and I really wish I was half as handsome.'

Her face wrinkled into a grimace. 'That's not what I mean. You and he have the same intensity, that same look in your eyes.'

By now, my laugh was contemptuous. 'I think the only thing Zaheer Khan has in common with me is that we are both prone to injury,' I said.

Dr Sood fell silent.

'Doctor, I really wanted to talk to you about something. For the last few days, all I seem to be able to think about is my abuse. I remember these little details I had altogether forgotten. I'm not sure if this is an effect of the depression, but these thoughts are plaguing me every day.'

The therapist looked down and asked, 'Have you ever thought about joining a gym, Shreevatsa?'

'You have me stumped,' I told her, shaken.

In July 2008, a year after I had been diagnosed, I desperately wanted to escape Bombay, and I used the bait of a master's degree to justify my move to Brighton.

Giving me sanction, Dr Joshi told my father, 'Dr Sood and I use Shreevatsa as an example when we meet other bipolar patients now. We can't think of anyone else who has recovered so quickly from a manic attack.'

My deliberate naivety made me think my psychiatrist meant 'cured' when he said 'recovered'. The side effects of the medicines he had prescribed had transformed bipolarity from a mental to a physical affliction. The lithium left me thirsty at all times, and I had lost my appetite for food and sex. Depakote, an anticonvulsant drug, exacerbated the tremor in my fingers and had caused my hairline to recede with urgent purpose. Together with olanzapine, an antipsychotic, these drugs made me perpetually drowsy, and in just twelve months, the cocktail had forced me to gain six kilos.

Packing my boxes, I decided I would reclaim my body. My recovery had come at a price I no longer wanted to pay.

A week before I left for Sussex, I met Julian Menezes, a Delhi University professor of English, whose iconoclasm and rectitude had corrected much of my undergraduate credulity. Sipping his third cup of chai, Julian looked up and said, 'I hope you know that bipolarity is only a pharmaceutical conspiracy.'

My curiosity was obviously piqued. 'I'd easily be convinced by such a theory, but what do you mean exactly?' I asked.

'Almost everyone I know has had one major bout of depression in their lives, and nearly all these people have once felt unduly energetic. A psychiatrist will look at them and conclude they're type-II bipolar. The diagnosis means they can write a prescription, and that means that pharmaceutical companies will be able to sell more of their drugs. Everyone gets a cut. Everyone is happy, except the unsuspecting patient who is swallowing these debilitating pills entirely uselessly.'

The trust I had placed in my doctors had been hard to muster, and Julian only diminished the authority of mental health practitioners by proving them corruptible.

'But I'm type-I bipolar, the original manic-depressive,' I protested. Julian patronized me with his wry smile. 'And who told you that,' he asked, 'the same man who insisted you start taking lithium and Depakote?'

When I called her from Heathrow, Lucia confessed she had a hunch she had tried not to voice. 'I don't think you are bipolar, Shev. I think the doctors in India got it all wrong. I think what you suffered was a one-time psychosis. I have been looking it up on the Internet and your symptoms fit perfectly.'

I dismissed her confidence—'I think that's just wishful thinking, Luce'—but as I then began to imitate Britain's immigrants, inventing a history that eliminated inconvenience, I believed my bipolarity was dispensable. Soon after I had stopped filling my pillboxes in October, my hands had stopped shaking and I was losing weight, but by Christmas, I was spending my days wrapped in a blanket, unable to read and write for college, surviving on takeaway pizza and cannabis.

My depression didn't take long to mutate into mania, and when I was taken to a Brighton therapist, raving and hysterical, I referred to Dr Joshi as a 'quack' and his diagnosis as a 'con'. I told Dr Donelson, 'I could decry the pharmaceutical nexus till the cows come home, but the system is always only a sum of its representatives, and Dr Joshi is its most despicable champion. What I had suffered was a one-time psychosis. Thanks to Dr Joshi, here I am, saddled with "bipolarity" for life. Such a misdiagnosis ought to be a criminal offence. Do you not think so?' The doctor could only nod.

A little over twenty-four hours later, I stood outside the Delhi airport, waiting for my cousin to chaperone me back into a family I felt I had recently forsaken. My mania had made me irate and itinerant.

Sitting in his passenger seat, I tried convincing Rana that together we could get rich, that I wanted to be a child rights activist—'There are some wrongs that are unpardonable'—and that I was weeks away from finishing my first novel. 'Before the world becomes our oyster,' he said, 'there is this doctor I need you to meet. It will only take a few minutes and then we have all the time to make something of ourselves.' Tucked away in an affluent corner of South Delhi, Dr Prakash Makhija had converted a bungalow into a hospital and de-addiction centre.

Sipping his tea, I castigated Dr Joshi again. 'He has ruined my life with his prescriptions,' I shouted.

I fell asleep on the couch, and when I woke up, I found myself tethered, my hands again tied to a hospital bed, my feet numb.

The injections Dr Makhija's nurses administered and the pills they forced in my mouth did nothing to mitigate my mania. Even a week after I had been admitted, I still could not read the clock. Thinking it was five in the evening, I knocked on the door of a recovering alcoholic at dawn, asking if he wanted to play Scrabble. At seven in the morning, I found the security personnel of the hospital had not woken up yet.

In an escape I thought was cinematic, I climbed the centre's high gates. The spikes and barbwire left me bloody and bruised, but sprinting down the streets of New Friends Colony, I tasted a freedom which, though transient, was exhilarating. It took six men to drag me back. As I kicked and screamed, the tarmac further grazed the wounds of my palms and thighs. This time, the orderlies tied both my hands and my feet. I was refused cigarettes when I began using them to burn the back of my hands. In the three weeks I was in his care, I hardly ever saw Dr Makhija. Seeing I was reading again, my parents saw hope in my brief moments of lucidity.

Left with a six-figure bill on the day of my release, my father said, 'We were taken for a ride.'

I snapped, 'I bet you enjoyed that damn ride far more than I did.' I returned to Calcutta to break ashtrays and porcelain. My mania was obstinate.

Renowned in Calcutta for his 'bipolar success rate', Dr Abhijan Ganguly was the next doctor I met, on a grey March afternoon in 2009. With pictures of gods and their devotees hanging from its every wall, his chamber resembled a Hindu shrine. When I told him I was tired of drugs and their many side effects, he played an air piano and said, 'The point here is to make your mind harmonious, at one with the universe.'

Leaving his clinic, I told my parents, 'I need a psychiatrist, not a shaman.'

~

My mother's reaction to my madness is invariably physical. She breaks into a fever, she suffers palpitations and is then forced to survive an unrelenting insomnia that sadly matches mine. Even after seven weeks, my mania was proving impossible to mollify, and my mother's need for a doctor seemed more urgent than mine.

Seeing Dr Bharatendu Madeka remove his shoes in our passageway one day, I looked at my father and asked, 'Is this one an executioner or an exorcist?'

He was irritable. 'This one's for your mother.'

Though I do always return to my childhood when I am manic, I also find joy in rediscovering the temerity of my adolescence. As music blared from the speakers in my room, the smell of my many cigarettes filling our house, I heard a knock on my door. Dr Madeka asked in a hushed voice, 'Shreevatsa, can we talk for a minute or two?' The general practitioner had an unusual manner. He sat on my bed, put his phone away and scanned the spines of books I had stacked on the floor of my room. 'You obviously like to read. What are you reading now?'

Elated that someone had finally taken an interest in my reading habits, I went and sat next to him. 'I'm actually reading ten books simultaneously. It's amazing how they all connect to each other.'

Dr Madeka's laughter was convivial. 'Isn't that what they mean when they say comparative literature?'

Dr Madeka, I found, was easy to warm to. I told him, 'I feel like devouring everything I see, doctor—books, music, films, newspapers, people, everything.' He smiled and asked, 'Would you say that this appetite has increased of late?' His few questions were not an inquisition.

'Something happened when I was in Brighton. I think it's what the scriptures describe as enlightenment. For the past few weeks, everything has been resplendent. It's like I can suddenly tell light from dark.'

Dr Madeka nodded his head empathetically. 'We live in a state of mystics. The experience you describe certainly does have precedents, but this illumination can sometimes make us forget that we have to continue living in society, that there are people we are responsible for, there are parents who care for us.'

I felt anger creep into my voice again. 'My parents do this each time. Each time I am on the verge of a realization that is momentous, they throw me into a hospital and strap me to a bed, like some animal that is a danger to the entire zoo. And none of this humiliation helps. I don't think I need to apologize or atone for how I think, for who I am.'

Dr Madeka opted for philosophy over pragmatism. 'If I were to ask who you are, what would you say?'

I said, 'I am Kalki, looking for my white horse.'

After having indulged my delusions for another half hour, the affable doctor looked me in the eye and said, 'Shreevatsa, I need you to acknowledge a single fact. At this point, you are high. This fact doesn't discount anything you have seen or come to know, but you have to bring yourself down a few notches, and you need to do this for yourself and the people around you.'

Rather than rebel against Dr Madeka's imploration, I found myself unexpectedly pliant. No one had ever treated my mania with such consideration. 'But I'm taking all these medicines,' I said.

'The mind is more wilful than you imagine. It will resist the strongest drugs if it wants to. You need to bring yourself down. You need to start living your life again.'

I quipped, 'At least my mind has free will,' and seeing the doctor smirk, I went on, 'I'll do anything you say, but I won't visit Dr Ganguly.'

Dr Madeka patted my back. 'I'm going to send you to a friend.' Feeling boundless gratitude, I told him, 'You do seem to have changed my life.' His final consolation was pithy. 'You must know that if this awareness you claim is true, it will survive.'

~

Years before I had volunteered to get my urine tested every month for the presence of cannabis in my body, I would abuse the substance on the sly. As marijuana skewed the arc of my mania, I would greedily buy and smoke it more. Terrified that my doctors would only cut off my supply of drugs and stem my mind's growth, I refused to visit them in my mania of 2013. The ferment I had assiduously manufactured forced me to quit my job in a huff. I had spent my savings buying aeroplane tickets impulsively, and was then borrowing money from friends and family to drink alcohol in luxury hotels and to bankroll my industrious peddler.

My aunt in Gurgaon had always been a benefactor, and on the evening of 16 June, I rang her doorbell, expecting my wallet to be filled. In her living room, I saw Dr Ishita Malik waiting with a male nurse and two lanky orderlies. 'Not this again,' I sighed out loud.

Looking at me squarely, Dr Ishita said, 'We're here from the Fortune Foundation, and we just wanted to speak to you for some time.'

I was already irate. 'You can cut out the routine. I know why you are here and you must know that I'm not going to go anywhere with you.' I walked to the door, only to find that it had been locked from the outside.

Seeing me pace from one end of the room to the other, the doctor went on, 'You haven't been yourself lately.'

I snapped. 'You don't know me, so you're in no position to make that call.'

The floral salwar kameez Dr Ishita wore covered her slender frame. Her mascara tried to hide the dark circles under her unusually big eyes. Though her lipstick was a shade too dark, I thought to myself, 'Too pretty to be a mental healthcare worker.' I banged my aunt's coffee table and said, 'I cannot see anything that's wrong with me. Please leave.'

Dr Ishita leant forward, grinding her small legs into the floor. 'Shreevatsa, look at how angry you are. Would you call this your normal behaviour?'

My hands on my hips, I said, 'If I am angry, I have reason to feel that way. I have been working for an organization which I've found is corrupt to the core. I have been taking medicines that leave me entirely numb, and at no point in my life have I been understood. All that together is cause enough.'

Her voice still even, she tried consoling me. 'We're here to understand you.'

I asked menacingly, 'Really, and what are your credentials?' She nodded in the direction of the nurse. 'We're all certified professionals here. You can rest assured of that.' I saw the nurse start to prepare a needle.

'Let me guess, your certificate is that syringe. I will not allow you to touch me with that.'

Running two fingers through her straight hair, Dr Ishita said, 'You have a choice. You can willingly choose to come with us.'

I was beginning to submit to the inevitable. 'How long will I have to stay with you?'

She said, 'At least until we can understand you.'

Located on the border that separates Delhi and Haryana, it didn't take us long to reach the premises of Fortune. A plush farmhouse that was doubling up as a drug rehabilitation centre and a mental healthcare facility, the walls around the institute's grounds were impossibly high. There would be no escape. Led to a large room that had been plastered with inspirational posters, I was asked to surrender my phone and my belt. The nurse was tapping his needle again, and I stood like Jesus, my arms outstretched on an invisible crucifix. As I was being injected with a deep yellow liquid, I looked to Dr Ishita. 'Even if I ask him, the Father will not forgive you. You really know not what you do.' I woke up in the basement the next morning, and finding me agitated, desperately looking for a way out, one of Fortune's twenty-one patients broke into song—'Hotel California'.

'You can check out any time you like, but you can never leave.' His mirth did little to calm my nerves.

Later that day, I was asked to join a group session that was being led by Dr Ishita. 'For those of us who are attending this class for the first time,' she said, looking at me, 'it is important to remember that to completely recover from addiction, we need to follow, to follow religiously, the twelve steps of the AA [Alcoholics Anonymous] recovery programme.'

Strangely obedient, my fellow inmates prefaced each of AA's steps by giving the group their names and repeating, 'I'm an addict.' The stringy man on Dr Ishita's left was excitable, and he stuttered when he said, 'We admitted we were powerless over alcohol—that our lives had become unmanageable.' An oddly reticent woman said, 'We made a decision to turn our will and our lives over to the care of God as we understood him,' and the twelfth member of the group recited proudly, 'Having had a spiritual awakening as the result of these steps, we tried to carry this message to addicts, and to practise these principles in all our affairs.' I felt I was part of an evangelical mass.

Having corrected the diction of the group's participants and filled in the blanks of their memory, Dr Ishita turned to me. 'It'll take you a while to learn these by heart, but for now, you could maybe just introduce yourself.' Feeling rebellious and indignant, I stood up and said, 'I am Shreevatsa. I am a journalist. I'm not an addict, and I'm certainly not a zealot. Thankfully, I'm not in school either.'

The doctor's eyes widened. I had crossed a line, and she was quaking with rage. She shouted, 'You're a journalist, so why don't you go read the papers upstairs? You'll be welcome here only after you have learnt some manners.'

I was glad to leave. For the next three days, I sat in Fortune's kitchen, read the papers, drank countless cups of

tea and befriended residents who'd all declared my defiance
to be legendary. A schizophrenic poet told me she had been
confined in Fortune for months because her paranoia had
become too cumbersome for her cousins. A dental student had
been interned because his parents had found some cannabis in
his room. Sharing my cigarette, a weak-willed artist finally told
me, 'This is jail, and like with any jail, you must remember that
sentences get reduced for good behaviour. I have now been here
thrice, but how do you think I get out each time? I comply.'

Though abrupt, this advice made my capitulation absolute.
If I had to be a student again, I would be diligent, and if I had
to be guilty, I would be repentant. Finding Dr Ishita sitting
alone in the glass-panelled therapist's enclosure, I walked in
with my head lowered. 'I know I'm reprehensible, but I'd
really like to apologize for my behaviour these past few days.'

Her lips broke into a half-smile. 'Finally, he comes
around.' Sitting opposite her, I said, 'I don't know what
came over me. I'm usually never like that.'

She leant back in her chair. 'It's fine. You're coming out
of your mania, but the sooner you realize that we have some
rules and regulations of our own, the better things are going
to be for you.'

I asked, 'Is one of the rules recognizing myself to be an
addict?' Dr Ishita looked me in the eye and said, 'But you *are*
an addict.'

I countered, 'I thought I was here because I was bipolar.'
She shook her head. 'We found twelve packets of marijuana
in your backpack. That would surely mark you as an addict.'
Staggered by the fact that my belongings had been searched, I
said, 'It is my mania that makes me turn to pot.'

Dr Ishita was smiling again. 'But it is the "pot" which makes you manic. I do have some bad news for you. You will always be an addict. Addiction has no cure. But while you're here, we'll try and ensure that you recover.'

I had come to think of Dr Ishita as overbearing and imperious, but that afternoon, her calm seemed conciliatory. I felt relaxed enough to ask, 'And will that therapy be psychoanalysis? I'd really like that.' She frowned and said, 'We don't follow Freud here. Besides, psychoanalysis takes too long. We'll be using CBT—cognitive behavioural therapy. What psychoanalysis takes years to do, CBT does in a matter of weeks.'

I was still curious.

'And what's the basic difference between the two approaches?'

Dr Ishita was now impatient. 'It's all a little too complicated to explain, but put simply, psychoanalysis will tell you that you're dysfunctional because of your negative experiences, whereas in CBT, we believe your behaviour is dysfunctional because your beliefs about who you are are distorted. It'll all become clear soon enough.'

Wanting to endear myself, I told her, 'You look like my sister.' She waved me away with her hand.

Dr Ishita brought her chihuahua to work every day, and it was Paw-Paw's diffident bark that would make me stub my cigarette, spray my deodorant and brush my teeth a second time. Clean and spiffy, I would plant myself in a spot Dr Ishita was sure to turn to. Her approval, I felt, was both my return ticket and my upgrade voucher. Ending another of her pedantic group sessions, she said, 'I'd like you all to write notes of gratitude from today. You need to learn some humility, so thank everyone you can think of.'

In a long ruled notebook, the kind which I had once used to list elementary particles and the dates of our Mughal history, I thanked my parents for a 'much clearer and less addled future', Fortune Foundation for 'tolerating my protests', and its compounder for 'tripling my dose of olanzapine'. A Jesuit education had taught me how to go down on my knees and thank the Lord, but it had also made obedience all the more difficult. I wrote, 'A certain part of me has stopped believing in the possibilities of a Higher Power, and for that, I think I have a Higher Power to thank.'

When Dr Ishita asked for my notebook to read, I gave it to her with an imp's trepidation. She circled the few instances of my insolence and then reached for a pen to write, 'God's plan for me comes true through honest openness and willingness.' The 'real' sins, she dictated, 'are assumption, grandiosity, confusion, blame, victimhood, entitlement and boredom'. I instantly counted seven. 'You know what,' she said angrily, 'this isn't working. From today, you'll keep a thought diary. Think of a situation and write it down. What mood does it leave you in? What's the automatic thought that comes to your mind? Note that and then you have to present the evidence that supports it and the evidence that doesn't. You'll then arrive at an alternative, more balanced thought. What action are you going to take to implement that? Write that down in the end.'

Considering the punishment too harsh, I said, 'This sounds like a scientist's procedure. Shouldn't thoughts be spared such drab observation?'

Dr Ishita scowled. 'Your first thought should be, "How do I correct my bad attitude?"'

My first few thought diary entries were dismissed by Dr Ishita as too abstract. 'I want to know how you will prevent a slip,' she said, 'not how you will gain confidence as a writer.'

Changing tack, I began to stress routine and exercise as a solution to all my problems, banal and philosophical. I even earned a smiley when I wrote, 'The only two words that would faithfully describe my time at Fortune are "progress" and "recovery". Even though it might not be easy at all times, I would never describe my days here as difficult or impossible.'

My submissiveness softened Dr Ishita. In our sixth one-on-one session, she said, 'You seem to have finally gotten off your high horse, so now would be a good time to talk about your bipolarity. When you're manic you want all or nothing. When you're depressed, you discount the positive. You magnify problems when you aren't manic, and when you are, you minimize them. You think you can read people's minds and you find yourself in everything.'

I confessed I checked each of those boxes. 'There's the catch!' she exclaimed. 'You think these are symptoms of an imbalance, but the mania and depression transpire because these are your core beliefs.'

Her fervour had begun to leave me nervous. 'But many of these beliefs are remnants from my childhood, and you know my history enough, it wasn't conventional.' Dr Ishita pressed her pruned eyebrows and said, 'We'll deal with your childhood another day, but you can't hide behind it forever. Your distortions are your problem, not your negative experience.' ✗

damaging (in-class)

Dr. Ishita

When Dr Ishita gave me a piece of cake on her birthday, I learnt she had turned twenty-eight and had graduated three years after I had. My fellow patients had begun winking in my direction each time she asked for my help when writing Fortune's brochures and fund applications.

Almost three months after she had brought me to Fortune in a car with tinted windows, I looked up from her laptop and said, 'You'd told me you'd talk to me about my abuse, doctor. It weighs heavily on me, and I can't tell you how indebted I'd be if you'd help.'

Asking me to sit on the chair next to hers, she said, 'I have a problem with the word "abuse". Did you ever say no to your abuser?'

I felt myself grow tense. 'No, I never did say no explicitly.'

She then asked, 'And this person was your cousin?'

I replied, 'Yes, I was eight and he was eighteen.'

She crossed her arms and said, 'What happened to you was incest, not abuse. You were a consenting partner.'

She reached for my notebook and wrote the question. 'Why are some individuals able to find closure and not others?' She then listed four possible answers below: (1) The content of the trauma event; (2) The intensity of the pain associated with the trauma; (3) The longevity of the trauma event; (4) Current association with individuals related to the trauma event.

'I think each of these answers apply to me,' I said timidly.

She smiled and wrote, 'These four points are NOT AT ALL RELATED to one's ability to find closure.' Faced with a theory that was radical, I was torn between its acceptance and dismissal. Though I had never undermined my participation in my abuse, I now came to feel a novel guilt. My abuse,

Dr Ishita was suggesting, was a construct. 'You tell yourself that you're a sensitive human being. You say, "Life has been so unfair to me. Nobody understands me, so I can smoke all the cannabis I want." You blow your pain out of proportion and you allow emotions to overpower you. You ask why you can't find closure. Well, because you don't want to.'

The tremor in my hands reached my legs. I was catatonic. I felt ridiculed and belittled, but more acutely, I felt penitent. 'What can I do to better this, doctor? How can I better myself?'

regret

Dr Ishita spoke in a voice that was uncharacteristically soft. 'You'll have to take small steps, but what you can do immediately is write a letter to your eight-year-old self and tell him how you feel at this point.'

She was fiddling with her phone when I returned half an hour later. I began to read my letter. 'Dear Bunshi, even though it feels repugnant to accept, I think the world of tactility that Satyah offered was a welcome relief to us. There remains a difference between abuse and incest, and even though I have, until now, identified what happened to us as "abuse", I am beginning to understand that "incest" would maybe describe our experience better because we were willing participants in the act, all through the four years.'

Dr Ishita walked in my direction and said, 'And don't you think Bunshi will ask you to remember that you didn't have to face the ordeal on a daily basis? A silver lining, no?'

The day I was being released, Dr Ishita called me to the therapist's glass enclosure and said, 'I didn't want you to leave. My work with you isn't done, but your parents insisted. I want you to practise everything you have learnt here. What would you say has been the most important lesson I've taught you?'

Shaking her hand, I said, 'That it's best to let sleeping dogs lie and that skeletons are best left in the cupboard.'

She joined my palms together. 'Skeletons are best left in graves. They have no place on the outside.'

For the first time in three months, Dr Ishita had said something more inventive than dangerous.

~

Over the years, there have been numerous occasions when I have entered Dr C.S. Mukherji's room defeated and depressed, but in 2009, on the first day we met, I was entirely disconsolate. The horror of my manic breakdown in Brighton had left me panicked, but the recollections of its violence had crippled me with shame. 'I have hurt the people around me, doctor, and the damage, I feel, is irreparable. I don't think I'll ever be able to earn their forgiveness,' I told him. Sitting beside me, nervous and afraid, my mother added, 'And he has been irresponsible, doctor, especially when he was away in England.'

Dr Mukherji looked at her with some disapproval and said, 'I'd like you to wait outside, Mrs Nevatia. I'd like to speak to Shreevatsa alone.'

Having discovered a rare agency, my bipolarity suddenly free of parental supervision, I outlined the drama of my history for the next twenty minutes. 'I first felt something shift when my grandmother passed away in 2004,' I said. 'I was facilitating a writing workshop when I went manic for the first time in 2007, and I have always wondered if I have language and literature to blame for my bipolarity.'

Dr Mukherji smiled. 'I think your lack of sleep may have been more culpable.'

I went on, 'And my mother is right, doctor. Cannabis is a problem.'

Dr Mukherji reached for some scrap paper, and drew a basic algebra graph with two axes, x and y. The wave he drew curved into high crests and then bottomed into steep troughs. 'Put simplistically, this is what the mood of a manic-depressive is like. Your mania is high enough to border on a dangerous ecstasy, and the lows, much like the one you're suffering now, convince you that there is nothing to look forward to.'

The second line which the doctor drew resembled a low tide, creeping upon a shore. 'This is what the mood of someone who isn't bipolar looks like, and this is the graph we would like your emotions to resemble. We do not want to eliminate joy and sadness from your life. There are good days and there are then those that aren't. We just want you to enjoy them for what they are.'

Dr Mukherji's enunciation and explication were equally delicate. Plotted with coordinates, my condition seemed simpler to grasp.

'I've always been prone to overreaction,' I confessed. He suggested regular therapy with Dr Pushpa Misra, and medicines to control my moods. I shook my hand and pleaded, 'Please, no Depakote, doctor. It takes away all feeling.' Filling his prescription pad, he said, 'I'll keep you on just the lithium. You'll have fewer pills to buy.'

My mother was sullen on the ride back home. She had been told I could fill my own pillboxes. My bipolarity was mine to manage, and for the first time in two years, this control gave me back a voice I had forgotten could be lucid. In my first few sessions with Dr Misra, I was effusive. I found on the shelves of the Freudian psychoanalyst a copy of Gabriel García Márquez's *One Hundred Years of Solitude*. 'Colonel Aureliano Buendia's father took him to discover ice, doctor,' I said, 'but mine used to take me to a Kali temple every Sunday to discover God.'

In a room drenched by the yellow light of a single lamp, I detected a feminist impulse in the Mahabharata and called myself an existentialist—'I want to be someone who is for himself, not in himself.' Weeks after I'd exhausted Dr Misra with my literary and mythological references, she asked, 'So what's your earliest memory?'

'I must have been four,' I told her. 'I had fallen into the habit of kissing my grandmother without pretext. I'd do it all the time. For various people, she was a gentle matriarch, someone they would come to for advice and counsel. This one day, we were sitting in our living room, surrounded by a group that had travelled all the way from Maharashtra to see her. I was pressed up beside her on the couch, and while she listened, I felt an irresistible urge to kiss her again. As my lips pressed against her cheek, she pushed me away with her arm and said sharply, "Not now. There's a time and place for everything." I don't think I will ever forget that.'

Dr Misra asked, 'How did that make you feel?'

I admitted I felt alone. 'It felt like I had lost her affection forever. I suddenly felt aware of an audience. I knew she did not just belong to me, that there was a world she was part of too.'

Wiping her glasses, my psychoanalyst said, 'You're aware that the drama you describe is profoundly Oedipal, right?'

I was distrustful. 'I'm not perverse, doctor.'

She smiled. 'No, this is common.'

Through several sessions, Dr Misra rid the Oedipus complex of its age-old moral scandal—'Desire is only misunderstood when taken too literally.' My negotiation of an early childhood wish—to be my grandmother's centre of attention—was arguably shoddy, and my sexual and psychic development, as a result, had been neurotic.

Delineating her application of Freud's theory, Dr Misra said, 'Each time you go manic, you cry for your grandmother, missing the plenitude of her affection. In moments more lucid, you will admit that you will never be able to reclaim that plenitude, yet you yearn for it, like a child would. You might want to accept that you, or at least a part of you, is refusing to grow up.'

Candid, sometimes to the point of being stern, my psychoanalyst has also always been compassionate. Recognizing my childhood to have been a site of trauma, she spent months encouraging me to revisit my abuse—'You can only forget what you've once remembered.'

Though I often felt anxious and overwrought when recounting the events of my abuse, the very telling of my best-kept secrets enabled an unburdening that was curative. Talking about the violence of my sexual initiation helped me locate its pain and pleasures in a distant past. Of course, the effects of that abuse, as I complained to Dr Misra, were perpetual. 'I have forever felt afraid and guilty. I am always deferential because I feel I need to apologize for a thousand faults. I'm always afraid I am doing something wrong, that one day I will be caught.'

Having heard me out with her trademark patience, my psychoanalyst said, 'You need to consider the possibility that the person judging you is your conscience, not anyone else. There's a term we often employ in psychoanalytic parlance—the "superego". This is the self-critical aspect of the ego, the aspect which judges the ego's demands and helps it come to terms with reality. In your case, your abuse forced your superego to invent a moral standard you then felt you could never live up to, and you're still a prisoner of those expectations. When you're manic, you're narcissistic, and you expect the world to live up to those moral and social standards you've created, and when you're depressed, you are again racked with fear and guilt because those ideals, you find, are impossible for you and the world. It's a cycle you have to break.'

The logic of Dr Misra's reason was immediately compelling. 'I don't want to live like this any more, doctor, and the more I think about it, the more I feel the need to escape my abuse, to stop it from defining me. But I do need to ask—do I need to forgive to be free? Is it essential?'

She looked at me solicitously and said, 'It is essential only if you want some peace of mind.'

~

A few days later, resolved to liberate myself from malevolence, I went to meet Satyah for the first time in a decade. I sat cross-legged on his mattress and we talked about the weather and the latest Hollywood release. Like me, he too had grown a paunch. He chewed tobacco, and he tried to shush his wife when she told me he had grown addicted to television. I stared at his moustache. I had not mustered enough courage to look him in the eye.

In a corner of his room, I saw strips of medicines stacked neatly on a tray. 'It's funny how you and I are in the same boat,' I told him. 'I find it hard to leave my room sometimes. Do you ever get the same feeling?' I asked.

'We're brothers,' he smiled. 'We've got the same leaks.'

We laughed with some abandon, and before leaving, I held him close and gave him an inordinately long hug. 'We should do this more often,' he said. 'There's a lot of lost time we need to make up for,' I concurred.

Later that evening, I called Dr Misra and Dr Mukherji. Exaggerating the length of our embrace, I said excitedly, 'I did it! I built a bridge. I forgave Satyah.' Though delighted, my doctors stopped short of calling this absolution a breakthrough. My next bout of mania sadly brought with it the same hatred I thought I had forsaken, but for a few weeks, I discovered in pardon a wholly unexpected lightness.

~

Almost every time I am manic, I bring out from my cupboard a long black kurta, convinced it will absorb all the light and heat I need. Familiar with my few wardrobe predilections, Dr Mukherji laughed as I once entered his room in 2011. 'I see the black robes are out again,' he said.

Still expansive, my mania gave my thoughts a telltale levity. 'It doesn't matter who or what I look at, I feel as if I am encountering myself,' I told the doctor. 'You might find that phenomenology comes to the same conclusion. I could recommend a few books if you'd like,' he said.

Even as he upped the dose of my mood stabilizers, he prescribed reading more, not less. Despite the hubbub of his busy waiting room, Dr Mukherji has always taken three-quarters of an hour out of his schedule to talk to me about my work, the tumult of my romantic relationships and the new books I have bought for my shelves. My moods have found an unusual validity in our exchanges. Every three months, my blood is tested to gauge the level of lithium in my body. But more than my blood work, it is in language that he has found symptoms make themselves apparent.

9

We Need to Talk about Shreevatsa

W hen one is manic, even the most ordinary meal can come to seem like the Last Supper. In February 2016, eating a Chinese dinner with friends in a Calcutta restaurant, I waited for something momentous to happen, a betrayal or at least a miracle.

Taking our order, the waiters looked restless. Our table of six would be the last to leave. Their faces fell when one of us said, 'A friend is yet to join us.'

Eating with an astonishing relish, I was distracted from my main course by the shouts of a drunken customer who was standing at the door of the eatery's kitchen.

'How could there not be enough salt in the food?' The man grabbed the jacket of the cowering chef and screamed, 'How dare you?'

I had seen enough. That evening, my vigilantism did not need a mask. And the meek, I was resolved, must inherit the earth. I stood up, straightened my shoulders and marched up to the punk. Tapping him on his built biceps, I asked, 'Is there a problem here?' He turned his face from the chef and said, 'No, there's no problem. Why don't you mind your business?'

I raised my voice. 'I would if you let me. If it weren't for you, we'd be enjoying a quiet meal here.' Seeing him glare and quake, the drunk's three friends, two of them burly and beefy, decided to intervene. They dragged him outside.

I followed them out and standing on the pavement, having lit a cigarette, I saw the unruly diner being mollified. 'Of all the sins in this world, entitlement is the most despicable. If you haven't been taught how to behave in public, you really shouldn't be allowed to eat out,' I shouted.

Shubho, I saw from the corner of my eye, had finally arrived and was on the phone. Glad that my heroism again had an audience, I went on, 'If it's a fight you're looking for, why don't you pick on someone your own size?'

I was about to roll up my sleeves when Shubho came and whispered in my ear, 'Go inside. I got this.' It took him a few minutes to diffuse the situation and offer an explanation on my behalf. He paid for my meal, and after the restaurant's chef and staff had hailed me as their protector, he looked at me and said, 'I'll drop you home.'

Soon after we sat in his car, Shubho asked, 'How do you think that would've turned out?'

I was still irate. 'We'd have found out if you hadn't intervened,' I said.

'You really think you would have been able to take on those four men all by yourself?'

Not stopping to consider the pragmatism of my friend's caution, I replied, 'If it came to that, yes, I would.'

He pressed on. 'You do know that no good can come of this recklessness?'

My courage had left me fearless. 'I can't just sit around watching people bully the weak into submission. I'm sorry, but I will just have to act,' I said.

'And you want to do this by putting yourself in harm's way?' Shubho asked.

'If I have to, it's a small price to pay,' I retorted.

'This gallantry is new,' he replied.

Thinking I had picked up on a touch of sarcasm, I let my annoyance show. 'Isn't everything?' I snapped.

'For you, yes, but for those around you, adapting to this new you takes time.'

Feeling claustrophobic, I said, 'I wish they'd hurry up because this "me" isn't going to change.'

Shubho went on. 'You've said this before.'

I sulked. 'It's best I shut up then.'

Love has often made me only more difficult.

Ever since we were sixteen, Shubho has been my rescuer. I was a philistine when he bought me a ticket to my first Hindustani classical recital and taught me how to eat lobster. I was still struggling to become a reader when he introduced me to the literature of Ian McEwan. He has seen me fall in love half a dozen times, and each time my relationships have soured, he has helped me rediscover felicity. Proofing my early journalistic writing and fiction, he underlined the value of brevity and made me aspire to an unadorned prose. In 2006, hearing me gush about the title Umberto Eco had given a collection of his essays—'How to Travel with a Salmon'—he had said, 'I think you should call your first book "How to Travel Light".'

When we were still in college, Shubho took me to the parties he was invited to, and I was soon included in his circle of acquaintances and friends. Each time I have gone manic, he has known most of those who have had to suffer an excess of my ardour, aggression and affection. As I lay in mental health institutions, pinned by the guilt of my transgressions, it was always Shubho who has cleaned the mess I left behind.

I started parading an intelligence and wit I felt I had come to possess when I first lost sleep in 2007. We were twenty-three. Standing at a busy Calcutta street crossing, Shubho looked to me and said, 'You must know you're already good at what you do. You don't have to prove anything to anyone.'

I soon broke ties with family. In the six weeks I was undiagnosed and unfettered, distance collapsed as quickly as judgement, and I found myself boarding a flight every other day. The next time Shubho found me, I was in Bombay, asking every rickshaw driver his name, staring women in the eye and confessing undying love to acquaintances and strangers in Bandra's bars. He was the first to find a credible psychologist and take me for an appointment he had made. He was there when Dr Joshi's ambulance came to take me away, and weeks later when I had returned to Calcutta, penitent and surly, Shubho would visit every day. My melancholy never dampened his ebullience, and in his constant presence, I found assurance. I had not lost my friends.

When convinced I had exhausted an earlier capacity for levity and invention, Shubho's conviviality gave me hope that my ability to think and laugh could be continuous.

He took me for a walk when my mania again became manifest in 2011. 'There comes a point when your mind itches to disintegrate. You have to stop that from happening,' he said.

I gave him my phone. 'I shouldn't have this then.'

Recurring after two-year intervals, my mania regrettably made the cycles of my moods predictable, and by 2013, these spells only interrupted the now adult lives of those around me. Workdays would have to accommodate my sudden phone calls and the news of my distress. I had begun to disturb meetings and disrupt schedules. Empathy, I imagine, would come tinged with frustration. Oblivious to how cumbersome my madness had become, I had again taken to smoking cannabis with a teenage abandon.

Seeing me take a drag of a joint that was being passed around the room, Shubho asked, 'Do your doctors know?' Bluster, I thought, was my best defence. 'Of course they do,' I lied.

'So you're telling me that they're fine with you smoking pot?'

Wanting to resist control, I said, 'You should try googling "marijuana" and "bipolar". There are enough studies which prove that cannabis regulates bipolar moods. I've done my research.'

Shubho wasn't prepared to back down. 'We have the theory of your research and the evidence of your past.'

I returned to Delhi to exhaust the last of my goodwill. Having quit my job, I was castigating my employers, and when I'd turn up at the houses of friends and family unannounced, I'd borrow money to feed my habit and pay for private cars I'd hire to criss-cross the city.

After Shubho had warned our friends and sounded an alarm, I was forced to check my spending. To guarantee a future, I had to be removed from society, and it was again my friend who called mental health practitioners, finally leading my parents to the website of Fortune Foundation. Each time I am released from an institute, Shubho is the first person I call. Scared that my manic capriciousness would have caused me to irreparably damage our amity, I've apologized profusely on each of these occasions. His forgiveness has been unconditional.

On a diet of delusions, the voice of reason is often the first you want to muzzle. Mistaking his influence for authority, I have criticized, even offended Shubho. I have belittled his concern and insisted I want to map a trajectory that is mine alone. He has let me. Our relationship, however, has survived the strain of my mutinies, and our humour preserves the insouciance of our boyhood. As I trap myself in my series of reinventions, the voice of my friend has been a reminder that I need to be responsible for the sake of my support systems, that I used to be lucid once, and that I am only human and fallible. I have never taken his understanding for granted. I have felt saved by his steadfastness. There's Shubho. He's got this.

~

In July 2015, a few weeks after I had again moved to Bombay, Shubho found a flimsy pretext to call me. We gossiped about the ridiculous in the typically flippant fashion of our banter, and finally, a few minutes later, Shubho said, 'You sound fine to me.'

It didn't take me long to join the clear dots. I asked him, 'Did my parents put you up to this?'

Reluctantly, Shubho confessed, 'They think you might be manic.'

I was incensed. 'If they are wondering if I am manic, why can't they come ask me themselves?' It took me some time to realize my question had an obvious answer.

There was good reason why I had, at times, felt infantilized by Shubho's solicitude. Since my diagnosis, my parents had often made him their proxy. My mania followed a defined pattern. In the days of its early onset, I would invariably have long, funny and winding conversations with my mother at five in the morning. I would sneak up on my father and hug him from behind. This affection, though, would soon be punctured by sudden flares of an unforgiving rage. I would accuse my parents of apathy, neglect and even malice. I would demand that we separate, and I would insist I never wanted to see them again. Choosing exile over dependence, I would leave home. I would hit where it hurt. Finding me stubborn and inconsolable, my parents would call Shubho, hoping he would look out for me, wanting to get their messages through.

I'd usually shoot the messenger, but that day in July, I was lucid enough to say, 'I'm so sorry you had to go through this again. Please know you have nothing to worry about. I'm fine. This time, I really can handle things.'

The disagreement I had had with my parents the day before would have been forgettable had I not lost my temper in the heat of an argument. I didn't approve of a business decision my father had made, and while letting my displeasure be known, I had said brusquely, 'I want to have nothing to do with this or any other such plan of yours. I really am done with you.'

Disavowal, in the eyes of my parents, was a symptom, and my anger was proof that a meltdown was around the corner.

'Does this mean that I can never be angry?' I asked Dr Misra, having decided to call her before I called my parents to confront them.

'It's a good thing you're letting your anger show in moments when you are not manic. We avoid that whole pressure cooker situation,' she said. 'But think about it. You're never angry in your daily life. You're always docile, always finding middle ground. Your parents might have justifiably gotten a little spooked.'

I was still annoyed. 'But this panic will only make things worse, and if this arrangement of my living away has to work, they really should be able to talk to me.'

My analyst agreed. 'You're right. They should be able to talk to you when they are concerned, but I also see why they are scared.'

Letting my self-pity show, I asked, 'I'm not that monstrous, am I, doctor?'

She said, 'No, it's just that they are scared of the monsters that once hid under your bed.'

~

I was twenty when I first told my mother I had been abused as a child. 'It all happened years ago, Ma, and I know that family can be very fragile, so I don't expect you to do anything about it, but I just thought this is something you should know.'

My mother stared into the distance unblinkingly for what seemed like hours, and when I confessed her silence was worrying me, she broke down and said, 'I'm so sorry. I'm really so very sorry. I couldn't protect you. I've let you down. Please forgive me. Please.'

Parents response [handwritten in top-left margin]

My father wrote me a moving letter in which he apologized for not having been there enough. 'I wasn't there when you were suffering the most. I didn't read the signs. Nothing I do can ever make up for the past, but I promise your future will never be so traumatic.'

My revelation surprisingly brought me closer to my parents in the summer of 2003. In their attentiveness, I felt I'd discovered closure. Mania, though, arrived to unstitch this togetherness and scratch our wounds.

Four years after I felt I had given my chapter of abuse a happy ending, I woke my parents up in the middle of the night and screamed, 'The person who stands by and lets a crime happen is as guilty as the person who commits it. And this crime went on for four years! For four years, you were oblivious to my pain, and even after I had told you about Satyah, you did nothing. You did not confront him. You let things be. You did not keep him away from children. Do you think that's just? But I am not here to ask for justice. I am here to deliver it.'

blame [handwritten in right margin]

Having given my speech, I stuffed some books and a toothbrush into a bag and left the house, as if to never return. After being played out thrice over, this scene has now become a cliché, and the prodigal son, my sister had once teased me, always returns.

Each time my parents have come to take me away from a Fortune or a Starlight, they have brushed my hostility under the carpet. They have forgiven me and discounted my recriminations. Relieved that my hate had not drained their love, I have quickly returned to being obedient and doting. Though the periphery of my relationship with my parents has

parents love [handwritten at bottom]

come to be defined by guilt, it is inevitably my shame that keeps me in line. I never want to hurt them again.

In 2016, having just been released from Starlight, I sat next to my mother on the flight from Bombay to Calcutta. 'I think I really let things get away from me this time,' I told her.

She held my hand and said, 'We're in our sixties, Shreevatsa. We are getting old. We really are.' I have since walked the line and kept my nose clean.

~

My favourite T-shirt as a ten-year-old was orange, but having been worn every other day, it had faded considerably. Getting dressed for a cousin's birthday party, I pulled it out of my cupboard again, as expected.

My mother walked in to see me spray the T-shirt with my father's cologne. 'You're not going to leave the house wearing that.'

Usually dutiful, I chose that day to stage my first rebellion. 'This is exactly what I will wear. Let's see you do something about it.'

Taken aback by my out-of-character mulishness, she tried relying on reason. 'There'll be people there. My relatives will be there. What will they think?' The T-shirt she chose for me was pink, and even though I muttered 'I hate you' under my breath while changing, in that moment I became aware someone was always looking, interested in how I had turned out. It is this gaze that surrounds me when I am manic, and it is that very gaze I turn away from when I am depressed. For much of my life, I had seen myself from the outside. My mother's question—'What will they think?'—became a private incantation, and wanting to survive the judgement of others, wanting verdicts to be favourable, I made myself likeable.

Hoping I would study law, my mother would use my school holidays to list the many perks of a lawyer's life. 'You'll be able to fly all the time,' she'd say. In an unconscious attempt to fulfil her once urgent desire, I now book myself several air tickets within days of turning manic. Flying from Calcutta to Bombay in the February of 2016, climbing a hysterical high, I found my mother's cousin standing near the plane's galley.

'So what are you up to these days?' he asked.

I was unemployed and my lies were prompt. 'I'm a media consultant.'

He looked impressed. 'And what does that entail?'

I leant against the washroom door and said, 'We consult media houses on how to make content relevant and profitable.'

My uncle soon sent my mother a text, saying he was glad to have bumped into me. My fiction, I prided myself, had had the desired effect. I'd made my mother happy.

A few months after my mother had made me change my T-shirt, I learnt the meaning of the word 'class'. Eating breakfast, I asked my parents, 'So what class do we belong to?'

Sipping his morning tea, my father said, 'We're middle class.' My mother glared at him. 'We're certainly not middle class. Don't mislead the child.' I was still puzzled. 'Then what are we?' I asked. 'Upper middle class,' my mother said.

'Yes, say you're upper middle class,' my father told me, stifling a laugh.

Three years later, my mother took to retailing sarees in an effort to prove wrong her husband's complacency and scoff.

Her industry made sure we had as many luxuries as we did comforts. She has paid the inordinately large bills hospitals and rehabs have left us with, and she has also been forced to fund the exorbitance of my mania. My depression after a typical episode makes work impossible, and in this time of recovery, my mother pays for my cigarettes, lithium and therapy.

I am usually in a rush to repay the debt of her beneficence, and I quickly leave Calcutta to find employment in cities that afford more opportunities. Though I start from scratch, my autonomy comes coupled with the desire to make perpetual the standard of living my parents enjoy.

Looking at my bank statement, my father had once said, 'You're earning more than I ever did.' I had held a job for six months, and my satisfaction soon came to border on rapture. A few days later, I was manic. Strangely, I always have at least a month's salary in the bank when I start unravelling. Having lived up to an ideal of financial sufficiency I had carved for myself, having earned my parents' respect and that of their family, I feel I'm left without a goal that can keep me on the straight and narrow. I can splurge in the five-star hotels my father used to take me to as a child and I can buy the Mont Blanc he had always coveted. In the first stages of mania, I always act out a facile interpretation of my parents' fantasies. I am dapper and articulate, affluent and generous, entrepreneurial and worldly. It doesn't take long for my savings to dry up, and faced with the bottom of my mother's purse, I again rage against her and my father's authority. The economics of my bipolarity, I've found, hinges on the extravagance of my childhood demands and the unforeseen limits of my adult supply.

~

My mother never did like *Silver Linings Playbook* very much. 'I live this life. I don't need to see it on screen,' she moaned. My father, however, was more impassioned. 'You get to be Bradley Cooper,' he told me, 'but I get to be Robert De Niro. I get the better deal.'

The film, it was clear, had hit home. Pat Solitano, the film's protagonist, is bipolar, and having pummelled his wife's lover, he has been interned at the Baltimore Psychiatric Facility for eight months. The day his mother, Dolores, goes to get him released, a doctor warns her, 'He's just getting used to the routine here.' Immediately protective, she says, 'I don't want him to get used to the routine here.'

Pat will have to live with her and Pat Sr, and Dolores tries her best to dampen the tension between father and son with home-made sandwiches and a frown. My mother knows well the frown that mixes anxiety and fortitude. Dolores takes Pat to therapy—'You can't live with us and not go'—and gets him to swallow his medicines. Faced with my obstinacy, my mother mastered her own tricks of persuasion.

Dolores sets Pat up with Tiffany. She calls Tiffany and tells her when and where Pat will be running. My mother, on the other hand, has been oddly circumspect about my affairs. 'For six months, you'll love someone with all you have, and then one day, you'll wake up wanting "space". I wouldn't want any girl to go through that. Why do you think I haven't gotten you married yet?' Her caution, though, usually withers the minute I start dating.

The day she finds me on the phone for an hour or more, she asks, 'So are you going to marry her?'

I can't help but smile. 'Ma, make your mind up, do you want me to get married or not?'

Sheepishly, she replies, 'No, I don't, but you know there's always hope, there's always a "what if"'

My father, for his part, is forthright. Like Pat Sr, his interrogations are more frequent. 'So, what's going on between you two?' he asks. 'Are you guys going steady? Can I hear wedding bells?'

I have often found myself impatient. 'What's this obsession with weddings, Dad?'

His answer is predictable. 'I need to know there'll be someone to look after you when we're gone.'

My father is as religious as Pat Sr is superstitious. Both are obsessive about order and both suffer the juvenility of their grown sons. Pat routinely wakes up his parents in the middle of the night. He once wants to know why Ernest Hemingway did not give *A Farewell to Arms* the happy ending its characters deserved, and then, a few nights later, he wants them to find his wedding video. I too have often not let my father sleep. He is my audience when I have chanced upon ideas that tie our minds together. He has heard me complain about the world's injustices, and he has, at times, had to survive my nocturnal fury. Though my father aspires to be De Niro, his composure is at odds with Pat Sr's volatility. Like him, my father is always looking for ways to keep me home and out of trouble.

Even though *Silver Linings* has been criticized for its candyflossed coating of the bipolar condition, it touches upon a thinly theorized encumbrance—having to live with your parents as an adult. A manic-depressive's moods ought to be monitored by his or her support system, but this supervision can come to seem like surveillance. Pat is asked where he's going each time he leaves home. One day when he wakes up feeling happy, his father asks, 'What are you so up about? Are you taking the proper dosage of your medication?' Few of Pat's emotions are free of Pat Sr's discerning gaze.

Recuperating in my parents' thirteenth-floor Calcutta apartment, I inevitably find myself avoiding friends and acquaintances for weeks. I hardly leave my room. In the winter of 2016, however, the weather had lifted my depression, and I had started staying out more. One night, I returned home at twelve-thirty to find my father waiting for me. 'Have you seen what time it is?' he asked.

'I have, and have you seen how old I am?' I was going to let my displeasure show. 'Wait, but if I say something, you're going to think I'm manic.'

My father sat on my bed. 'You don't remember all that you say when you're manic,' he said.

'The strange thing is I do, and there is not a day that goes by when I don't regret saying all that I have.'

I could see my father was worried. 'But you don't mean what you say. We know that.'

Choked, I said, 'That does not stop me from atoning for each of those sins.'

My father held my knee with his hand. 'There are no sins. There needn't be any atonement.'

'I just think if I take back all that I said, you wouldn't be this worried about me all the time. You wouldn't be up waiting for me, for instance.'

There was concern in his voice when he said, 'Me staying up has nothing to do with what you've said.'

'But you do stay up because I am bipolar, right? Isn't that worse?'

My father straightened up to say, 'That's something that is hard for me to forget.'

'But I take my medicines when I should. I sleep for at least seven hours a day. What more would you have me do?'

He paused for a second. 'It is our job to map the fluctuations of your moods.'

'But you make me feel like a rat in a laboratory. My moods seem to determine everyone else's. When I'm happy, everyone is cheerful. When I'm not, everyone at the dinner table is sullen. That's just too much pressure.'

My father looked at me and said, 'Maybe we can together find a way to be happy again, all of us.'

I paraphrased a dialogue from a film I had once seen. 'Why don't we just try and find a way of being all right with whomever and whatever we are? I think I'm really buckling under the stress of being happy all the time.'

My father lifted me by the hand and giving me a hug, he said, 'Get some sleep.'

I held him close and said, 'I am not that. I am not him. I am not him at all.'

~

Family has always been important to my parents. Through my childhood and early adolescence, they forced me to travel the country with them and attend the weddings of relatives I would never know. In Kanpur, where a distant uncle was getting married, my grand-aunt had given her two Alsatians typically fearsome names—Rocky and Rambo. Standing in her garden, my cousin, my sister and I stared in fear as the hounds were being taken out for their evening walk. Shreepriya, twelve years old and the oldest among us, bit her nails nervously. Radhika, all of ten, held her cousin's hand, and as an eight-year-old, I stood cowering behind them. Thinking us to be playthings, Rocky and Rambo barked maniacally. We were too frightened to move, and then suddenly our worst fear came true. The dogs escaped their leash and charged towards us.

My sisters ran into the house and locked the door behind them. They stood with their noses pressed against a tall glass window, watching me flail my arms and scream 'open up, open up'. They were too scared to act. For the next few minutes, they saw me run around in circles, Rocky and Rambo snapping at my heels. By the time their handlers had again restrained them, I had tears rolling down my cheeks and my heart beat furiously. As a manic adult, I still tend to run around in circles. The only difference is that my sisters now keep their doors open.

Shreepriya now lives in Bombay and Radhika in Delhi. Since I invariably choose these cities as theatres to perform my madness, they have together been witness to each of my crazed episodes. Nostalgia, they know, is a symptom. Calling them several times, I reminisce about the times they used to paint my nails and then hide the nail polish remover. I ask Radhika to again mimic characters from the Mahabharata, and when I turn up at their doorsteps, they make me the milk tea and toast that my grandmother would feed me on the sly before I left for school. Invariably, I fall asleep on their beds. Not just an antidote to my insomnia, their affection is also, at times, a cure for my frenzy.

On 28 February 2016, an hour after I had broken down on the phone, Shreepriya called back. 'Shivvy, you can't do this to yourself. My eight-year-old daughter heard you wailing, and she wants to know what's wrong. I realize things have been hard for you, and trust me, I know your pain, but I have two kids now. They adore you, and for their sake, you have to bring yourself back.'

Suddenly aware of a responsibility I had altogether forgotten, I promised, 'I'll be good. I will. I know what you're saying.'

Late that night, she sent me a surprisingly long text. She wrote, 'Please take your meds and sleep. I beg of you. Take your pills and get a hold of your life. Don't neglect yourself. You really need to sleep to come out of your high. You are playing with fire by not taking your medication. I don't want you to land yourself in a mess again. You are thirty-two, no longer a child, Shreevatsa. Please take some responsibility and take care of yourself. You have to come out of this high. I'm saying this for your own good. I don't want you to suffer.'

I replied, 'I love you, more than this world.'

Her response was typically sisterly. 'Cut the crap. Take the meds.'

That night, when Starlight's bouncer rang the bell, I opened the door expectantly. I wanted Shreepriya and my milk tea.

When Radhika came to meet me with her husband in the Fortune farmhouse, a schizophrenic inmate stood in front of us with his hands tucked inside his trousers. He drank the Coke she had brought me and had eaten half our pasta.

My cousin turned to me and asked, 'Are you all right here?' I nodded and said, 'As all right as I can be.'

Her small baby face twisted into a frown. 'I'm not going to let you be in a place like this again. Besides, I have never seen what the problem is with your mania. You might be more effusive, but you're still my little brother, you're still fun.'

Her protectiveness made me talkative. 'That's only because when I'm with you, I never feel any need to be aggressive. I wish that was true for everyone else I met.'

She smiled and said, 'Everyone cannot be me. I'm special.' For the first time in weeks, I laughed unaffectedly.

When she finds I have spent all my savings, Radhika has always insisted I take her money to meet my expenses. If she sees I have updated my Facebook status after midnight, she immediately calls to ask, 'Bitch, why haven't you slept yet? Are you taking your medicines?'

I allow my sisters an authority I often deny other members of my support system. Their fuss is a rare source of comfort and their bullying never comes laced with hostility. I turn to Radhika when my heart gets broken. In Shreepriya's occasional control, I come to relish the protection family affords.

'You're very screwed up,' Shreepriya told me once, 'but you dare screw things up again! Mania gives you your kicks, I know that. You enjoy it, but then it's that same mania which gets you locked up, which gets you depressed. It is just not worth it.'

I smirked. 'Who made you so smart?'

She walked across the room and smacked me on the head. 'You behave or you'll have me to deal with.'

~

Growing up, I was always an object of ridicule for Shreepriya; as all siblings perhaps are to each other, at some point, growing up. She mocked my ambition and stripped me of my pretences. When I was thirteen, I announced, 'Natty and I are writing a book. It's set in Congo. It's about lions, and we have decided to call it "Fatal Attempt".' My sister looked up from her Danielle Steel and said, 'That's exactly what your book will be—a fatal attempt. I will die if you ever try making me read it.'

All my life, I have tried to read every book Natty has. We were in the seventh standard when I discovered Richard Bach and Paulo Coelho, but Natty, ever wise and discerning, had already graduated to Herman Hesse and Jack Kerouac. Together, we wanted to join the great rucksack revolution and be dharma bums. We wanted to climb mountains and pray. We said we'd make children laugh and old men glad. We especially wanted to make girls happy and women happier.

One afternoon, walking up our school's steps, I told my best friend, 'Sometimes I ask—what if I am Vishnu, sleeping on my serpent? Doesn't the world come alive only when I open my eyes? What if reality is nothing but my imagination?'

Years later, Natty would put to rest my metaphysical worries by saying, 'I finally know what I hate about your mania—this habit you have of making yourself the centre of every narrative.'

Manic and undiagnosed, convinced I had found a key to unlock the secrets of Márquez and Kundera, I'd spend my nights walking the streets of Calcutta in the summer of 2007. Natty once decided to join me. In the early hours of the morning, he saw me jump on pavements and devise theories

I felt were radical. 'Physics and Mikhail Bakhtin come to the same conclusion. There are two forces—centripetal and centrifugal. The centripetal force moves you to the centre. It is the force that seeks to regulate us and our language. The centrifugal force wants to break away and create a multiplicity. I am that centrifugal force.'

I told him I was here to turn the world upside down. 'I want the world to be a carnival where the courtier is the jester and the jester is the king.' Natty did not dismiss my ravings. He heard me out patiently. The universe, I said, explains itself even in billboards. I pointed to one that showed a child doing a cartwheel. 'See what I mean?' I asked.

Natty looked at me with some alarm and said, 'Now that is just going too far. That really is going too far.'

A few days later, I called him and said, 'I've left home. I need a place to stay. Help, will you?' He found me in a bookshop, excited again. Milan Kundera had just published a collection of essays—*The Curtain*—and I held it up for him and read the line, 'In the theatre, a great action can only be born of some other great action.' Grinning inanely, I said, 'I think my great action just happened.'

Natty took me to a guest house he had convinced his father to rent. 'I don't have an issue with the dramatic, but do you know what you're doing?' he asked.

I didn't know better. 'It feels like a start.'

For over two decades, Natty and I have discussed Freud, Derrida, Coetzee and Camus, but our dialogue also makes space for the mythological, the absurd and the shallow. When I am depressed, our correspondence forces me to write again. When I am lucid, I feel compelled to show him all the drafts of my journalism, and on the occasions when I am manic, it is in our conversations that I give my racing thoughts some guise of measure. He never belittles my far-fetched constructs. I survive in the world, and sometimes thrive in it, because he indulges my incoherence when I am at my worst.

Natty gives my euphoria and my melancholy equal credence. In literature, theory and cinema, he finds for me metaphors and allegories that explain my condition, and rather than pose hurdles to my fancy, he plays along with my madness. Once when I was depressed, he'd said, 'I don't see why I need to treat you differently when you're manic. Books and movies will be your death, not bipolarity.' His forbearance can never be a right, but it is an ideal for me.

After Natty moved to Europe in 2008, our exchange has mostly been limited to long emails and longer phone calls. Minutes before I walked into a job interview in 2009, scared my bipolarity will cost me the position, Natty mailed to say, 'I am no historicist, but may you come into your own during the interview.' In 2013, worried that my bipolarity had left me penniless, he wrote, 'Word on the street is Delhi is becoming frivolous. This is my way of asking without being silly, how are you doing for cash?' I have given him my many passwords, hoping he'd monitor my online tomfoolery. He has only asked me to curb the velocity of my language. 'We do not want another accident.'

Having just watched Quentin Tarantino's *The Hateful Eight*, we had much to talk about in the January of 2016. Trying to find a parallel, another narrative where bodies were dispensable and violence inevitable, we started discussing the

Bhagavad Gita. 'Now that's an instance of a failed text,' I told Natty.

'Do you mean the prose? Don't pretend you know Sanskrit.'

I giggled. 'I'm not that manic yet. But think about it, Krishna spends all this time trying to convince Arjuna he should fight. Much of the text is a compilation of lists. Krishna points to all life forms, and says, "I am this. I am that." The prince, however, is unconvinced. And then Krishna is forced to reveal his multi-armed form, the joker in his pack. "I become Death, the Destroyer of Worlds." Arjuna is so scared he'd do anything at that point. Dying in battle is a far better fate than seeing death itself. Language, though, has failed, no? You can skip the book and go to the last line.'

Natty laughed and said, 'But you can say that for any book.'

I chuckled.

Acknowledgements

Suryapratim Roy, without whom no page of this book would have ever been written.

Nandini Nair first asked me to write about my experience of bipolarity for *Open* magazine. She gave me my voice. She has edited my writing and my thoughts, giving me hope that I too can talk pretty one day.

Dr Pushpa Misra and Dr C.S. Mukherji have treated me for eight years. Their patience helped me survive the excess of mania and the paralysis of depression. Their generosity has given me my language.

Dr Gita Dore and Bhavya Dore suffered the indecision of my early drafts. Without their encouragement and critique, I would not have found the pluck to persevere.

Aakanksha Gupta helped me go pro each time the going got weird. She made this memoir possible.

Meenal Baghel set a standard for me to match, and her early feedback helped me discover audacity.

Aditya Sinha, for all the second chances he has given me, and for always saying it like it is.

Sahana Ghosh offered affection and inputs that bettered both me and my writing.

Kumkum Dasgupta made herself available when I needed counsel. In her suggestions, I found solace.

Arunabha Deb gave this book its title. He has also, on numerous occasions, given me my sanity.

Rajni George and her team at Penguin Random House India put more faith in me than I deserved. In Rajni, I found an editor whose kindness never once flinched. I would never be able to thank her enough.